· *Advance Praise for* ·

LET'S GO WIN!

"Most ache to win, yet struggle, wondering how. JM lives in a way that guarantees it and teaches his every secret here. No doubt the lives who take hold of this tool and use it accordingly will experience a transformation that will awaken a new level of success and fulfillment. Written with excellence and timed to perfection, with an undeniable mix of humor and heart, this one is one for the record books. Dive in—your best life and greatest breakthroughs await. Thank you, JM, for this treasure! A must-read!"

—**DANELLE DELGADO**, *The Millionaire Maker, Business Strategist*

"JM Ryerson has nailed it! JM lives this book in his daily life, and the results he has seen are undeniable. The chapters on vulnerability, intention, and accountability made me a true believer. The ease of his writing, simplicity of the plan, and powerful evidence he puts forth make this a must-read for all!"

—**DON SPINI**, *author of the #1 bestselling book,* 60-Seconds to Yes

"*Let's Go Win* is a must-read for anyone who wants to go to the next level in their personal and professional life. JM has done a beautiful job of taking the reader on an introspective journey of transparency and vulnerability that is inspiring and refreshing. He makes you feel as if you are not alone and that anything is possible."

—**ENDYIA KINNEY-STERNS**, *award-winning television executive producer,*
CEO, All Things Media Inc.

"I really had fun reading this book! It's full of wisdom and heartfelt thoughts I can apply to my own life! Now, I am more excited to pursue my dreams as I share this with my team!"

—TARO ARAI, *Chief Dreaming Officer, Mikuni Restaurant Group, Inc.*

"I found myself constantly nodding along as I read *Let's Go Win*. JM's advice is straightforward and practical, and also accessible to anyone, regardless of where you are on your journey. Everyone can learn from this book."

—AARON BROCK, *Executive Director of Missoula Food Bank & Community Center*

"Very motivational. JM has taken complicated concepts and made it easy to use them for your business. I strongly recommend reading this book if you're building a business and recruiting."

—MIKE DUNCAN, *30-year insurance and investment business veteran, Vice President, National Life Group*

"*Let's Go Win* is an essential guide for living a more meaningful and fulfilling life. JM Ryerson has captured the elements needed to maintain happiness and success."

—NISHA E. BACCHUS, ESQ., *president of The Bacchus Law Firm and Florida Women's Law Center*

LET'S GO WIN!

LET'S

THE KEYS TO LIVING

GO

YOUR BEST LIFE

WIN!

JM Ryerson

For information or to order, please contact:

Let's Go Win
735 Sunrise Ave #212
Roseville, CA 95661
916-900-2675
Email: Lisa@letsgowin.com or JM@letsgowin.com

WWW.LETSGOWIN.COM

ISBN: 978-0-9800406-2-3
First Edition
Copyright © by Let's Go Win

Cover and interior design by Marisa Jackson

Printed in the USA

· DEDICATION ·

For Trey, TJ, and Lisa.

ACKNOWLEDGMENTS

I believe in practicing gratitude daily and have done my best to include everyone here who has been a coach, mentor, guide, and friend through the years:

To my ghostwriter and project manager, Jennifer Lill Brown, while those titles are technically accurate, you do so much more, and this book would not exist without you. I have thoroughly enjoyed this process and look forward to the next one, as I greatly miss our weekly talks. Also, thanks to Jen's entire team, from book design to editing. How easy you all made this process!

To Danelle Delgado and Ben Jerome, for your various and numerous contributions to this book. Danelle, for making it clear that I was selfish if I didn't write the book and share it with the world. Ben, for reading every draft along the way and providing great insight. Your willingness to be a selfless leader astounds me.

To my business partners for always listening to me drone on about some new ideas from a book, podcast, or thought leader. Chris Reid, you are still the most loyal, hardworking guy I know. There are too many others to mention, but please know that you have forever changed my life for the better.

To my friends, who have always been there and allowed me to be completely vulnerable as my most authentic self, including my boys in Montana and my Appreciation Financial family. I also want to recognize those who have made California feel like home for the past two decades and the countless other individuals who have impacted and shaped my life.

To the many authors whose books I have read. Reading has been a massive part of my development, but a few authors that stand out from the crowd are Viktor Frankl, Malcolm Gladwell, Carol Dweck, Simon Sinek, Charles Duhigg, Patrick Lencioni, Brené Brown, and Adam Grant. These and so many more have served as mentors, provided new perspectives, and inspired me to win every day!

To my parents, Doug and Lynn Ryerson, thank you for your guidance, always being there, always believing in me, and loving me no matter what. To my siblings for all the years of laughter, tears, support, and love.

To my boys, Tristan and Treytan, you are the inspiration for this book, and you give me purpose every day to show up to be my very best. I love you both more than you will ever know!

To my wife, Lisa, for always putting up with me and loving me no matter what. You make me better with your love, guidance, support, and radical transparency. I love our life, and you will always be my Special Lady Friend!

TABLE OF CONTENTS

"The two most
important requirements
for major success are:
first, being in the right
place at the right time,
and second, doing
something about it."
RAY KROC

TIMING IS EVERYTHING

A funny thing happens when you tell other people you are writing a book. Nine times out of ten, they will respond with, "Oh, I've *always* wanted to write a book!"

The reason for this shared desire is actually pretty simple:

We are all living lives that are full of big lessons, great wins, colossal failures, and path-altering moments.

The things we learn from each win and each misstep, so many of us feel compelled to pass along—perhaps in the hope that others will sidestep some of the disappointment and get straight to the good stuff.

At some point in your life, I imagine you've thought, "What if I could help my kids (or grandkids, nieces, nephews, friends) avoid a few of the pitfalls and climb higher than I ever could with my knowledge as their guide?"

I am no different. I started this journey with a simple goal: to ensure all of the lessons I learned from my parents, grandparents, mentors, books, and life experiences would be documented and passed along to my children.

My wife and I fervently wish to provide our kids with the best possible chance of winning and having a better life than we could even dream of for them.

My career and my existence have been lived in overdrive in an attempt to wring every bit of knowledge out of this short time we have on Earth. In recent years, some of the most influential people in my life have made it clear that it is my duty and obligation to see the bigger picture and share what I have learned with more than just my kids.

But why me? I'm not a scholar, professional athlete, or movie star. I haven't invented a revolutionary device, and I can't travel through time. I don't perform life-saving surgeries, and I have no idea when flying cars will become our primary mode of transportation.

I'm just . . . me.

My life is not perfect, nor do I claim it to be. I'm constantly working on these very lessons. But I've found that living my best life happens when I attempt to incorporate the 12 key elements within this book into my day.

So, why did this book really come about? Maybe it's because people that I love finally convinced me to stop being selfish.

Or maybe it's just the right time.

I don't believe there are many coincidences in life. Whether we want to believe it or not, life is intentional in its path. I have found this to be true, time and time again. I have also found so much truth in this saying that originates in Tibetan Buddhism: "When the student is ready, the teacher will appear."

Many of the valuable lessons my parents tried to impart to me over the years fell on deaf ears, perhaps because of the stupidity of my teenage years—but also maybe because it wasn't the right time for me to learn those lessons.

Ultimately, I wasn't able to comprehend or even know how to apply the lessons when I first heard them.

It just wasn't the right time.

Wouldn't it be nice if we were always ready to heed the advice of our parents, our elders, and our coaches? It'd be ideal . . . but it's also unrealistic.

You will learn the lessons you need in due time—and for you, I hope that *now* is the time for you to hear and, I hope, absorb what I want to share with you.

During the past 20 years of coaching, leading, and teaching, I've noticed that no matter how important I think some lesson or training may be, there are plenty of people who just don't get it, or maybe just don't care.

Not everyone has to be on board! If I can affect just one person, then I have fulfilled what I have determined to do.

So, that brings us here, to this sentence, inside this book you now have in your hands. I want you to *win* in this life—and I believe the lessons I've learned along my journey so far can help you get there.

My humble intent is for these lessons to resonate with you and make a significant impact on your existence. Some of the ideas may seem simple—but who needs more complication in their lives?

If I have learned anything, it's that the simplest solution is almost certainly the right one.

I'd like to make one request before we continue, and that is for you to remain open to re-learning some of the lessons you thought you knew, so that you can open the doors of possibility in your life.

Real learning happens after we think we know it all.

Have you ever thought you knew it all? At some point, most of us do. So, before we begin, allow me to acknowledge the many people who taught me these lessons, even before I was ready or willing to learn them. To my family, friends, and mentors, I hope that my actions have shown you the gratitude I feel for each one of you in my heart.

I want to be intentional in everything I do on my path. For this reason, I designed this book to be a short-and-sweet, 12-step guide to winning—plain and simple. The end goal is to have a one-on-one conversation with you in much the same way we'd have if we were seated at a table together, or even sharing a bottle of wine over dinner.

My promise to you is to remain 100 percent authentic and genuine. I also promise to be vulnerable and give you all of my best efforts in order to provide the best experience possible.

If I may be so bold as to make one more request, it would be to ask that you give your best effort and be intentional in your application of these lessons.

There is absolutely no judgment—in fact, there is only a *celebration*—in allowing your genuine self to be vulnerable so you can get the most you can from this experience.

Thank you for joining me and being open to learning something new. I believe you will receive what you need from this book when the time is right.

Here's to the moments in life that shape us and help us win!

"Vulnerability
is the birthplace of
innovation, creativity,
and change."
DR. BRENÉ BROWN

· One ·

VULNERABILITY

I have read plenty of books on success and best business practices, and let me tell you one trait that is not at the top of enough lists of "must-have" qualities. Yet, it is the single most impactful trait that has rocked my reality, reshaped my priorities, and ultimately made the most profound difference in my life.

How I wish someone had told me sooner about the freedom and joy that comes from being *vulnerable*. Like most valuable lessons, I figured out its worth only through its absence for most of my life.

My first five years as a business owner were intense. I worked 90 hours a week and saw no end in sight. I'd set a goal, and come hell or high water, I would hit that goal with no regard for who might get hurt or what the consequences might be.

I just kept "grinding" because that's how I thought it was done. I was determined to keep my head down and push ahead until I received some signal that I had made it and could then sit back and enjoy the fruits of my labor.

What a surprise when things didn't work out as I imagined.

Don't get me wrong. My business was a success in the sense that we grew an average of 30 percent or more every year—and I'm certainly not discounting the importance of bottom-line results in business.

However, my line-item victories were achieved at the expense of many things including, but not limited to, nearly destroying my marriage, losing friendships, and betraying my most authentic self by losing sight of what should have mattered most.

I had been guilty of buying into the traditional idea that the path to becoming successful is fixed and one-dimensional. I thought I had to look and sound a particular way to achieve significance and to make my mark. I thought that the harder I pushed and the more callous I became, the faster the payoff would be.

While this might be a typical story for many entrepreneurs, just because something is *common* doesn't mean it's *healthy*. There is a much better way to work, live, and accomplish your goals.

The past ten years have been my most fulfilling *and* most successful decade. My marriage is whole and repaired, once-lost friendships are again on solid ground, my business is thriving, and I experience joy every single day.

So, what was the change?

I did the one thing that I'd been told *not* to do for years—I led with my heart. I became vulnerable, an open book of emotion and honesty.

If it sounds scary, you're not wrong. It can be. But the freedom that results from being vulnerable outweighs all that fear.

WE'VE GOT IT ALL WRONG

But wait a minute.

If you are open and authentic, terrible people will take advantage of you, right? *Maybe* you can get away with being vulnerable at home if you are already in a healthy relationship, but definitely not at work . . . right?

Whenever I speak about this principle, I am always ready to address this objection. I hear things like, "But JM, there are too many bad people in the world that will take advantage of you if you open up and trust too freely."

If you can relate to this, then again, you're not wrong. I am assuming (though I haven't personally met many) that there are lots of awful human beings in the world who are just waiting to swoop in and destroy you.

But those people aren't actually the problem here—the real issue is we equate *vulnerability* with *weakness* in this society.

The formal definition of vulnerable is "able to be easily hurt," while the definition of weakness is "the state or condition of lacking strength."

Those definitions are quite different from each other.

Just because you are capable of being hurt doesn't mean you are weak. You can be vulnerable *and* bold. In fact, being vulnerable is a bold choice! You can stand up for what you believe in and still remain open to honesty, love, and differing opinions without anyone naturally taking advantage of you.

One of my favorite authors and a leading expert on vulnerability is Dr. Brené Brown. Her 2010 TEDx Talk, "The Power of Vulnerability," is one of the ten most viewed TED Talks of all time and is definitely worth watching if you haven't seen it. I also highly recommend her *New York Times* bestselling book, *Daring Greatly*. I love her thoughts about the power of vulnerability:

> *"I spent a lot of years trying to outrun or outsmart vulnerability by making things certain and definite, black and white, good and bad. My inability to lean into the discomfort of vulnerability limited the fullness of those important experiences that are wrought with uncertainty: Love, belonging, trust, joy, and creativity, to name a few."*

"Lean into the discomfort of vulnerability" is a phrase that makes you think. Why is it so uncomfortable for us to even *consider* becoming vulnerable?

We're not going to dig into deeply rooted psychological programming, but let me just say this: from birth, we are basically taught that to fit in, we need to do what everyone else does and think how everyone else thinks.

For example, growing up, I was taught this supposed truth: *Boys don't cry*. Boys don't show emotion. We're supposed to suck it up or, my personal favorite, "man up" and never let it show when something is wrong.

Have you ever stopped and thought about that for a minute? Why *can't* boys cry? Who does that dictum hurt besides the young men who are expected to bottle up emotions rather than let their feelings be free?

What's worse is this lie is being fed to girls as well. Young women are now growing up believing if they want to "hang with the fellas" in business, they better toughen up.

It's all nonsense!

Society has gotten this one wrong. I have made and will continue to make my fair share of mistakes as a father, but I'll *never* tell my kids (or my team at work) not to openly share their hearts and their true intentions with others.

At some point in our youth, we slip on our first metaphorical mask and pretend to be someone we are not in order to be accepted. After a while, we stop taking those masks off altogether, and many of us live the rest of our lives betraying who we are at our core.

Has this done anyone any good? Maybe in the short term, but even then, I'd question any "good" that comes from being untrue to oneself.

If this is such a damaging way to be, why are we still living this way?

That's a great question—and I hate to spoil the surprise, but it's a question with no answer that is compelling enough to keep up the charade.

So, I say let's drop the pretense. We aren't fooling anyone, anyway.

WHAT DOES VULNERABILITY LOOK LIKE?

What does *vulnerable* really mean, and how do we live life with a greater level of vulnerability? "Capable of being physically or emotionally wounded" doesn't sound too much fun to me. No one is going to stand in line at a theme park for the "you might get wounded" ride, are they?

That's why I prefer to use a less formal definition of the word from *Urban Dictionary*, which is this:

"Being open and genuine about feelings of the heart, mind, body, and soul. Trust without self-judgment or fear of reaction and judgment from others."

To me, that description more properly summarizes the real intent of being vulnerable.

Here's an excellent way to better understand the power of vulnerability: Think about the last time you watched someone's acceptance speech at an awards ceremony. There are basically two types of people who step on stage. First, you have the polished speakers who sound impressive and look flawless. They pull out their scripted sheets and graciously thank the people they are supposed to acknowledge. They do a little bow with prayer hands, and everyone claps respectfully.

Then there are those who stand up and show genuine emotion that you can actually *feel* through the TV screen or from your seat in the audience. You feel their tears, their surprise, their humility, their happiness, and the sincerity of their heartfelt, unprepared words.

Whose words do we remember two weeks or two years later: the polished speakers or those who bare their soul?

We remember the honesty and the tears, not the rehearsed, robotic speeches.

Am I telling you to start crying more often? I'm not—unless you like the idea of crying more often. What I *am* suggesting is to remove whatever barriers tell you to look and act a certain way.

Brené Brown puts it best when she says being vulnerable is not a weakness but rather the most courageous thing a human being can do!

BEING VULNERABLE AT HOME

When I discuss this with others, most people can get on board with the idea that being vulnerable at home might benefit their personal life. Maybe that's because when it comes to our relationships, we need all the help we can get. For those of us who are married, were married, or are in a serious relationship, I think we can all agree that relationships are hard.

Like, really hard.

Imagine understanding *why* your significant other is upset or knowing what their true feelings are about something you said. That idea doesn't have to be science fiction. It can become the norm in your house when vulnerability is presented, accepted, and reciprocated.

How exhausting is it to wonder why your partner is giving you the cold shoulder? How refreshing it would be to know precisely what is wrong or what is bothering your partner?

Instead of trying to guess what is wrong (and if you are anything like me, guessing incorrectly), what if your partner openly shared his or her fears, feelings, and desires? When you can communicate how you feel, including your concerns and your desires, it stops the dreaded guessing game in its tracks.

What if you openly shared *your* feelings? Imagine asking for precisely what you need from your partner rather than being passive-aggressive about it—or worse, just plain aggressive?

How much happier and more fulfilled could you be as a partner, lover, and friend?

The answer is, a lot.

Now, here's the caveat: this is easy to say and a whole lot harder to actually do. It has been hard-wired in us to protect our hearts. In fact, if you ever want to wake a child, simply place your hand on their little chest directly above their heart and watch how quickly they awaken.

Quite literally, there is biology at play that tells us to protect our heart at all costs.

How would vulnerability impact the relationship you have with your children or the young people in your life? If you are a parent, you know that young children are the most vulnerable of us all. They give their love and their feelings so freely.

Is that such a bad thing? We never have to wonder why our kids are upset. They will gladly tell us—over and over again.

Why not give them the same honesty in return? Share your heart with your kids every day. Doing so will show them that it's okay for adults to reveal their feelings. We are allowed to have a bad day or to feel gloomy from time to time. We are also entitled to feel both immense joy and huge disappointment as a natural part of daily life.

BEING VULNERABLE AT WORK

Most people are willing to accept the idea that vulnerability can help their personal life. But can being vulnerable really help in business?

Absolutely.

Here is what I can say about my team: they *never* have to wonder what I am expecting from them. They never have to guess whether I think they are doing a great job or have areas where improvements need to be made. I share it all, openly and freely.

Even more than that, I don't pretend to feel great when I am having a rough day or struggling to feel positive. "Fake it 'til you make it" does not sit well with me. It feels too much like a mask, and masks are for parties.

False bravado and counterfeit strength only serve one purpose—they are façades that conceal the fact that you need encouragement and support. If you hide behind laughter and sarcasm when you are actually feeling weak and insecure, how will your team know you need help?

Just be real with people, and they will be real in return.

The unexpected and miraculous side effect of being vulnerable at work has been a dramatic increase in employee retention and overall job satisfaction for my team—and that's with no changes in salary and no corner-office upgrades.

It turns out that people like it when we remove our masks.

Be real and trust others—and your workplace will overflow with authentic connections and effective collaboration. When you work with people who trust each other, there is nothing you can't accomplish! You become bolder and braver together, and you start crushing goals that seemed daunting before you stopped trying to be an island of strength and grit.

An office that is rooted in vulnerability is an office filled with team members who don't send emails or make offhand remarks that are loaded with ulterior motives.

As John Mayer says, "Say what you need to say" because, why not? Life is too short for these ridiculous games we play.

Think for a moment about the way kids hug. Kids don't give weird side hugs or make awkward, stiff gestures when they meet a friend or see their parents. There is no holding back or disguising how happy children are. They wrap their arms around us tightly—they hug unreservedly!

Enthusiastically hugging your co-workers sounds like an HR nightmare, but I simply want you to consider the lack of pretense in the hug of a child. You can still work to give off the same kind of feeling in your daily greeting, a warm handshake, or a high five.

Greet, smile, and encourage unreservedly!

Another fantastic benefit of being vulnerable at work is it makes you a better teacher and speaker. I've trained my team both ways—with false bravado and with a sincere desire to help. Can you guess which one is more effective?

When you are speaking in front of a group, drop the pretense. What you wear, what you say, and definitely what you don't say (nonverbal communication) are all reliable indicators of how guarded your heart is.

MASKS ARE BORING (BUT YOU ARE NOT)

At this point, you may be wondering, "How will I know when I'm being vulnerable?" One critical element is undoubtedly the presence of mutual trust. Being vulnerable happens when you trust completely, and trust is returned.

With trust comes exposure, and that's the terrifying part for most of us. Yes, you are opening yourself up to potential pain, but you are also opening yourself up to healing and love.

Do you think that sounds corny? If you do, your mask may be doing too much of the thinking for you. Masks are boring, but here's something that is definitely *not* boring:

You are the only *you* that will ever be born. There is literally no one before or after you who will ever be the person you are.

Don't blow your chance to be you!

Whether you are vulnerable or not, there is still a distinct possibility you will get hurt in life. There is no such thing as a "safe space" where you will never be taken advantage of, lied to, or experience anything unpleasant. There are no guarantees that you will even wake up tomorrow! The amazing, bold, and inspirational Helen Keller put it like this:

> *"Security is mostly a superstition. It does not exist in nature, nor do the children of men as a whole experience it. Avoiding danger is no safer in the long run than outright exposure. Life is either a daring adventure, or nothing."*

Life can and *should* be a daring adventure!

As we move ahead to the next step, keep the principle of being vulnerable at the forefront of your mind. Without vulnerability, nothing else in this book matters.

Are you the kind of person who plays it safe? Do you have silent struggles and doubts that, if known, would embarrass you or make you feel inferior?

We all do. You are certainly not alone.

Tear down your walls and you may just find your most excellent adventure waiting for you on the other side.

I am not suggesting that you start telling your co-workers you love them or stand in a circle and sing Kumbaya while you all cry softly.

Just be you. Be sincere. Trust freely. Others will follow suit, and everyone will be far better off because of it.

LET'S GO WIN

"The goal is not
to do business with
everybody who needs
what you have.
The goal is to do business
with people who believe
what you believe."

SIMON SINEK

· *Two* ·

CULTURE

After I graduated from college, I did what I thought I was supposed to do. I went and found a job with a salary and a benefits package.

That's just what grown-ups do, right?

I soon found myself working 40 to 60 hours a week. The problem was, it didn't matter if I worked 42 hours or 60 hours—I made the same amount of money. That frustrated me immensely. I also found that no matter how much I tried to convince myself otherwise, working for someone else felt like I was clocking in at a J-O-B rather than building a rewarding career.

I grew up thinking that being a salaried employee with benefits was the only path. My dad had worked for the same company for 29 years, and my mom had been a teacher for 39 years.

Imagine my parents' surprise when I called them up one day to tell them that I had quit my stable, well-paying job to journey into the land of small business entrepreneurship. Here is how it went down:

"Hey, dad, I found a new career."

"That's great, son! What's your new salary?"

"Well, there is no salary."

"Oh. Well, the benefits must be incredible."

"Dad, there are no benefits. Not even insurance."

At first, there was only silence. Then, my father, who does *not* swear, finally spoke up. "JM, what the ★$!? are you doing?"

Like any great parent, he wanted me to make sound decisions that would make my life more comfortable and secure. Taking bold career risks is just not how he's wired.

Despite my parents' reservations, I continued on, and that became a life-defining decision for me. What caused me to strike out into the great unknown with no guaranteed salary and no 401k matching?

I wanted to create something that was my own.

I had spent my career up to that point feeling like a cog in someone else's wheel. I didn't know it at the time, but what I had been experiencing was a lack of alignment with the cultures in which I had been working.

Just because a company is respected and creates solutions for their customers, that doesn't guarantee the organization's values will align with your values. In fact, when you break it down, there are really only two kinds of cultures: There are cultures that make you excited to be a part of them, and there are those that rob you of your energy and ambition.

I was determined to find the kind of culture that made life feel less like work and more like a privilege. Maybe it wasn't possible, but I wanted to find out for myself.

FAILING UPWARDS

At first, after I had branched out on my own, I still didn't understand the importance of culture or really even what the word meant.

As a young professional, I had been inundated with too many traditional workplace ideas. I therefore believed that I had to look and talk a certain way, work a crazy number of hours, and remain hyper-focused on my goals to the detriment of everything and everyone else.

My first few years as an entrepreneur were filled with plenty of wins. However, those wins required far more effort than they should have. I was like a fish struggling to swim upstream. Thanks to the bravado and powerful professional mask I always wore, I was continually trying way too hard to be a guy I was not.

But you can't argue with results, right? The economy was buzzing, and people could not *wait* to hand over their money.

Then came 2008—the beginning of the worst economic recession in recent history. It was a period that revealed every flaw in virtually any business model.

What had once worked no longer did, despite all efforts.

The recession also brought to the surface the problem that many businesses face, which is when you expand quickly and experience financial success as a business, culture-building is often placed on the backburner.

"If it ain't broke, don't fix it," comes to mind. When you are making money, it's easy not to ask the tough questions or pick at the thread to see whether it might unravel.

However, without the proper culture in place at home and work, whatever wave you are riding will eventually reach the shore. I found myself grounded at the shoreline asking, "Now what?"

I had been relying solely on my willingness to work long hours and my relentless pursuit of the bottom line. I was forced to say, "This isn't working. It's time to figure out what I really stand for." Then I started answering some critical questions that should have been answered before I ever started, such as:

- Why does this business exist?
- Does my business culture resemble my home culture? Why or why not?
- What elements of my home culture can I transfer to work?
- How should working here make people feel?
- How should living in my home make my family members feel?
- How should doing business with us make our customers feel?
- What do I want to be known for in my professional life?
- What do I want my family to be known for?
- How can we win in *any* economic climate?

I had never fully considered any of these.

When you took away the masks I'd been wearing and the bottom-line pursuits, it was painfully evident that there wasn't much left. I had worked really hard and expected those around me to work hard, too—and that was about it.

Not exactly inspiring. And with increased financial pressures brought on by the recession, it wasn't enough for the business either.

I resolved to make some changes. First, I stripped away the pretense and started to become more vulnerable. Then, I began to do the work to figure out what it took, not just for me to win, but for everyone else around me to win as well.

The more I learned which elements make a winning *work* culture, the more I realized that those are the same aspects that make a winning *home* culture. We all want to be able to trust those around us. We want to have fun and laugh. We want chores and tasks to feel less like labor and more like privileges. We want to be heard, and we want to belong!

What kind of environment fosters growth and fulfillment for every person? I slowly began to find the answer to this question. That was when I more fully grasped the concept of culture and just how important it is for us to find where we truly belong.

THE QUEST TO BELONG

As human beings, we naturally search for identity. People of the same backgrounds and ethnicity seem to instinctively find each other to live and work together.

We want and need to belong.

Here's a great way to more fully understand this idea. Let's say you are in a foreign country, where no one speaks English. You're lost in a crowded plaza, and suddenly, you hear two people conversing in English.

How does that make you feel?

Such relief washes over you! You found people who can understand you—and, as a result, they can help you, you can help them, and you can bond over commonalities.

A distinct culture within your home and workplace functions in the same way. When you are surrounded by people who get you, life just works better. You speak each other's language. You can help each other, and you share a bond.

In this way, you all grow together. That's just how life tends to work. It could be language, background, sports or school allegiance, or work-place culture. Any of these can serve as a binding identity.

What we are talking about is building a thriving and healthy ethos, or culture. One of my favorite definitions of the word culture comes from author and former MIT professor Edgar Schein:

> *"Culture is the deeper level of underlying assumptions and beliefs that are shared by members of an organization, that operate unconsciously and define, in a basic 'taken for granted' fashion, an organization's view of its self and its environment."*

Your spouse and kids are going to feel a certain way at home. Why not do everything you can to ensure they feel loved and supported? The same idea applies at work. People are going to feel *something* about your company when they interact with it. Why not have some influence on those feelings by clearly defining the culture?

Don't just decide in your head what those feelings should be and assume people will get it through osmosis. Physically write down or type the key elements, print them out, post them everywhere, send them in an email, put them on your website, and remind employees at every staff meeting.

You should do the same thing at home. Sit down as a family and decide what your culture should be. Then come up with a few guidelines that the group mutually decides to abide by in the interest of creating a positive family culture.

Here is why this is so important: If you don't establish your core values in writing and make them known to everyone, you will inevitably become surrounded by people who do not align with these values.

The fact is, your culture is most clearly communicated through the people within it. The people *are* the company. A business will live or die not by some mission statement on the wall, but by its employees and what they bring with them into the organization. Similarly, your family will be known not by their words, but by their attitudes and actions.

Here's the deal. Life can be hard, and it is often more of a chore for people than a pleasure. You can change that at your workplace by developing a culture that gets people excited about coming to work (yes, that is possible). You can change that at home by collectively deciding what your core values are and staying true to those as a family.

Below are my four simple steps to cultivating a winning culture, a place where people are honored and excited to work, to live, and to play—an environment that naturally attracts the right energy and outcomes.

Remember, your goal is not to please everyone. You just need to find your people, and the only way to attract and create your own tribe is by consciously creating and transmitting your culture.

1. START WITH WHY.

When I'm coaching or mentoring people, and they tell me they are having trouble being consistent in their job, my first question is always, "Why are you in business?" If someone can't seem to stay motivated to get to the gym, I'll ask, "Why did you decide to start working out?" If a person confesses to feeling no joy in their marriage, my question is, "Why did you get married in the first place?"

For most people, their answers to this type of questioning go beyond superficial responses such as money, looking good, or loneliness. In fact, call me an eternal optimist, but I believe at our core, we are most contented when we are helping others, connecting with like-minded people, and developing into the best versions of ourselves. Happiness, health, and money are just bonuses!

When it comes to establishing a culture of consistency, the first step is to determine what matters, or your *why*.

Simon Sinek and his renowned bestselling book, *Start with Why,* serve as the gold standard for building a solid culture foundation. He teaches that our first focus should be on the why rather than any outward signs of success or happiness.

Skeptics like to point out that the bottom-line results are ultimately all that matter. In the sense that we all need money to pay our bills, put the kids through college, and support causes, I suppose that's true.

But isn't there more to life than chasing the next dollar or pursuing self-led interests? I'd certainly like to think so. Frankly, that sounds hollow—and since I've tried it both ways, I can tell you that focusing on your why is far more satisfying and a far better strategy for long-term happiness.

Building a why-based culture and pursuing success and happiness at work and home don't have to be mutually exclusive activities. In fact, they go hand in hand!

If you have never actively pursued creating a culture, then I'd like you to try this: Start digging. Ask yourself, "Why is _____ important to me?" Fill in the blank with work, your family, your health, your kids, or anything else, and then start answering that question honestly.

It's almost impossible to give 100 percent to something if you're not passionate about it. Find a reason that energizes you to give more. There are days when a job is just a job. There are days when sick kids and housework make you feel drained beyond belief. But, in the long term, if you're doing something you truly love—that is how you leave a legacy.

2. HELP OTHERS WIN IN *EVERY* AREA OF LIFE.

When it comes to establishing a healthy culture, it's essential to look at the big picture. Here is what I mean: At work, can you magically shut off all the other parts of your life? At home, can you miraculously turn off all thoughts about work?

Of course not.

The two are always going to intertwine. For this reason, I like to think of life as a puzzle with ten pieces. Absolutely everything we do affects another area of life, and they are all connected. Encourage everyone in your sphere of influence—from team members to family—to seek rounded wellness in all ten of these areas:

1. ***Spirituality.*** How do you fill your bucket? This could include religion or something as simple as quiet reading time, reflection, and meditation.

2. ***Health.*** Without our health, we really have nothing. How can we help each other make wise decisions in the areas of nutrition, exercise, and sleep habits?

3. ***Significant Other.*** The relationship with our significant other drives us to win or dooms us to fail. There really is no middle ground here.

4. ***Family.*** Are there any relationships with parents, kids, or siblings that need work? You never know what insight you may be able to provide to someone else who is struggling.

5. ***Friends.*** We all need friends, people who we can laugh with! If a co-worker doesn't have many friends, then you have found an instant way to help another human being.

6. ***Mission.*** Do you feel fulfilled by the work your company does? If not, what's missing and what can you do about it? Does your family have a unified mission statement? If not, can you create one?

7. ***Finances.*** I encourage my family and co-workers to be wise stewards of their money, and you can do the same. Because it matters.

8. ***Energy.*** What areas from this list are bringing your energy levels down? Are you struggling with health issues or something deeper?

9. ***Emotion.*** We are all allowed to have a bad day. But, don't let a bad day become a bad week. Help each other out of

slumps and get to the bottom of a depressed mood before it poisons the well.

10. **Adventure.** Encourage everyone to seek adventure! That could be in the form of a hobby, a vacation, or just a weekend hike. Get out and live life as the great adventure it is!

When one part is missing, you cannot see or understand the full picture. Help those around you find their missing pieces, and you will help your home and work environments become places of trust, comfort, and freedom.

I always say, "People don't care what you know until they know that you care." You could be the smartest person in the world, but if you don't genuinely care, your messages and your values will never be fully received or heard.

3. BE RADICALLY TRANSPARENT.

When I started becoming more vulnerable, I opened myself up completely and hid nothing. I am now an open book with no concealed agendas. In a sense, everyone has an agenda—some are positive (as in helping others win) and some are negative (as in helping only yourself to win).

Self-focused, hidden agendas are the problem.

It can be scary to become an open book. Being vulnerable means that you are now capable of being hurt or taken advantage of—but for me, it's now the only way I know how to operate.

I call this part of culture "radical transparency," which is a phrase coined by billionaire Ray Dalio. What you see is what you get and nothing more—and, let me tell you, this works for the people around me! My family and my team love the ability to be themselves. Ed Catmull, the former president of Pixar Studios, says, "A hallmark of a healthy culture is that its people feel free to share ideas, opinions, and criticisms. Lack of candor, if unchecked, ultimately leads to dysfunctional environments."

When you promote radical transparency, the full spectrum of human emotion becomes available. People can undoubtedly experience some lows, but they can also experience massive highs! They can also experience the freedom of not having to wear a mask.

My family sees me at my best and worst. So does my team, and they still love me. They respect and cheer me on regardless—and that is worth something that money could never buy.

4. SET EXPECTATIONS.

This part of the plan is not as sexy or inspiring as the others. But wow, it *is* crucial.

A lot of online chatter today suggests that the younger generations don't have a good work ethic.

In my experience, it's not about age, gender, or anything else.

It's about expectations.

At work, do a thorough enough job explaining the culture and the expectations that are placed on new hires from the start, and people may surprise you by rising up to meet you where you are. At home, let your kids know that just because their friends can behave a certain way, that doesn't mean it will work with the culture your family has created.

Children and adults alike actually *crave* order and discipline.

Your culture dictates what you allow and what you do not. You can enjoy a fun, inspiring environment and still hold those around you to high standards. However, those around you also need to be held accountable when their actions are out of alignment with the culture.

Call it tough love if you want, but you do it because you genuinely care.

If we all get on board, if we feel and think the same way, it just works. Otherwise, your career will always feel like a J-O-B, and your home life will eventually feel like an obligation rather than a pleasure.

Your culture will foster either victims or contributors. Victims place blame, while contributors accept their role in an outcome. You get to choose which type you attract! It's all about setting expectations and instilling a culture of accountability—and that starts with setting expectations.

THE CULTURE TAKEAWAY

I love this quote by Brian Chesky, co-founder and CEO of Airbnb, because I feel it perfectly summarizes the takeaway here:

> *"Why is culture so important? Here is a simple way to frame it: When the culture is strong, you can trust everyone to do the right thing."*

Developing a distinct culture is not a panacea for every issue you will face at home or work, but it *can* remove a lot of mistrust and go a long way toward making life energizing and rewarding.

The "find a job you love, and you'll never have to work a day in your life" quote is often misunderstood. People like to joke and say if we did only what we loved, we'd all be lying on a beach sipping piña coladas.

To me, that's not it at all.

The idea is to find something that matters—and then do it well.

Intentionally surround yourself with people who lift you up, and then lift them up in return.

Define the experience you want to live, and then live it.

Establish that you are not content to only see the world for what it is, but for what it *could* be.

Life is not always going to be sunshine and rainbows. But why not strive for fulfillment of your true vision?

LET'S GO WIN

"The definition of genius is taking the complex and making it simple."

ALBERT EINSTEIN

Three

SIMPLICITY

There is a motto that rules the minds of advertisers and marketers in today's loud, busy world, and it is this: "Complicate to profit."

The idea is if you make a problem seem so complicated that it becomes confusing and stress-inducing, people will gladly line up to buy your remedy to their pain.

You see this a lot in the health and fitness world. Fitness giants intentionally complicate things to convince people they need to buy a particular product, piece of equipment, or expensive program. Failure to adhere to a rigorous and product-intense schedule will only lead to disappointment.

On the other hand, fitness fanatics will tell you that it is only by simplifying the complex that they can reach their goals. In fact, the secret to being fit and healthy is pretty simple: Eat clean and move more.

That's about as complicated as it needs to get.

Yet, we buy the lie that all that "stuff" will get us where we need to be. Spend enough money on the right programs and products, and you can *buy* success, fitness, happiness, or results.

Well, I have my own motto that I live by: "The simplest way is always the best way."

I can't take credit for this concept since it's been around for ages. In fact, there was a concept presented sometime in the 14th century that is the foundation for all scientific theory building called Occam's Razor, which effectively states that simpler solutions are more likely to be correct than complex ones.

In a nutshell, this means that in science (and in life), the more complicated you make something, the less effective it will be at solving a problem or actually working effectively.

Modern life has become needlessly complicated. The way we schedule our days. The way we communicate. It's so easy to get overwhelmed with acquiring, learning, using, and doing all the stuff of life.

But when you boil it down, it's all just noise.

The world may complicate to profit . . .

But you can *simplify* to win.

THE GREAT EQUALIZER

One of my superpowers is taking the complex and breaking it down into bite-sized pieces. I'll take that ability any day over having the highest IQ. I am not usually the smartest person in the room, but I couldn't care less. In fact, sometimes natural intelligence seems to hinder a person's ability to see things through a more simplified, straightforward lens.

I once worked with a really bright guy who could talk circles around the rest of us about virtually everything. The thing is, whenever he would try to explain something, his explanation was so complicated that no one ever understood what he was saying.

He would get frustrated, and the expression on his face always said, "How are you *not* getting this?"

It's not that we were dumb, and it's not that we just couldn't get it. What may seem easy to some may simply be confusing to others. If you have to work too hard to get your message understood, something is wrong with the way you are saying it, not with your audience.

Well, here's the good news:

Simplicity is the great equalizer.

People of every IQ, background, and education level can understand the same message when it is conveyed in the simplest way possible.

No matter how intelligent or learned you are, it is human nature to drift in and out of the present moment. The more simply you can deliver a message, the more likely it is to get through—regardless of whether your audience is your spouse or a room full of 1,000 people.

Keep it simple, and people will stay engaged.

In the rest of this chapter, we'll cover my three straightforward steps to keeping it simple, both at home and at work. Using these guidelines will help you communicate in a direct, authentic way and get results that will enable everyone to win.

1. ASK THE QUESTION.

No doubt you have heard the adage, "Too many cooks spoil the broth." The idea is that when too many people work on something that *should* be simple, they tend to ruin it.

At some point in your life, you've probably seen a manual, whether an employee handbook or a furniture assembly instruction booklet, and thought, "That is needlessly complex."

Complexity and wordiness are sometimes due to legal requirements, but other times, it is the result of too many cooks in the kitchen. Trying to ensure every voice is heard, inputted, and reflected is not always realistic or effective.

The same idea is true at home. Think about the last time your family had the "Where should we go to dinner?" conversation. When everyone throws out their suggestion and no one can agree on one place, you are actually worse off than when you started.

Perhaps even more often, complicated or confusing policies and procedures are the result of a failure to ask the single most important question before you start a new task, write an email, conduct a meeting, or set out to achieve anything. Before you begin, you must ask yourself:

What am I trying to accomplish?

Instead of getting emotional or allowing everyone to bombard a discussion with contradictory ideas, ask the big question first and set the right tone and expectations.

In the end, the result may include a lot of moving parts, and there may be many people involved in its creation. But, as long as each piece is assembled intentionally to be in alignment with the one question, the probability of success will increase exponentially.

Amazon gets it right, which is why they are Amazon. They have taken one of the most convoluted things about business—customer service policy—and made it so simple. You need a refund on a product? They give it to you immediately. Not a refundable product? It doesn't matter. They will refund you with no questions asked because it makes sense to treat you, their valued customer, properly and keep you happy.

Making things overly complicated and losing sight of the one question can erode relationships, both business and personal.

If you care, keep it simple.

2. NEVER ASSUME.

When it comes to personal relationships at home or individual relationships at work, the question you need to ask is a little different, but still leads to the same conclusion:

Clarity.

If something feels wrong, but you can't figure out why, just ask!

The human brain likes order, and it tries to make sense out of life by placing people into convenient boxes. It may *seem* more straightforward to use labels for people, but in reality, that only complicates things because it obscures true motives and feelings.

Never assume you understand the underlying reason driving a particular behavior, attitude, or action. There is always more to the story than our rushed, emotional assumptions presume.

If you've done a good job of establishing an atmosphere of vulnerability at work and at home, you are likely to get an honest answer when you sincerely ask, "What's wrong?" or say, "Let's get to the bottom of this."

Most of the time, the answer is surprisingly straightforward. Your spouse may just be tired. Your kids might not be feeling their best or just got a low grade on a test. A person may not be an underperformer but dealing with a sick parent or child. He or she may not have the right training or could be confused about a particular aspect of the job. Or an employee may simply not be in the correct position that best highlights his or her skill sets.

The only way to know for sure is to ask!

Even if the solution is not simple, the path to that solution *can* be simple.

Let's say a person is underperforming at work. Well, there are a finite number of reasons for underperformance going back to the ten puzzle pieces in the previous chapter. One or more of those things is probably out of balance or missing altogether.

Labels don't work to accomplish anything other than create false assumptions and a lack of authenticity. Don't be quick to label someone as "lazy" or "unmotivated" before you dig to find what motivates and de-motivates them. Ask questions from a place of sincerity and expect honest answers. Then, make decisions based on what you actually hear, not what you *think* you heard or what you assumed.

It's that simple.

3. TRUTH IS ALWAYS THE SIMPLEST APPROACH.

When it comes to simplicity, no other word cuts to the heart of the concept more than "truth."

Do you remember when you were a kid and told a lie to your parents? Such lies typically required another lie. And then another. And another. In the end, you had this jumble of lies that were so complex you couldn't keep the story straight.

We don't have to remember what the truth is if it's the truth. Why pretend to know something or someone when we really don't? Why say we've read the book everyone's talking about when we actually haven't?

Now, you still need tact. Honesty doesn't have to be brutal. You can be truthful but also kind. In fact, it's imperative if you want people to trust you and remain open to what you have to say.

When you wear masks or pretend to be someone you are not, the truth eventually comes out. Save yourself some time and a whole lot of effort and just be you from the start! Act in a way that says, "This is who I am. You will like me, or you may not. Either way is fine."

Present yourself as you really are, and you will naturally find yourself surrounded by people who think and act as you do. If you've never tried it, you'll find it to be liberating!

The old saying, "The truth will set you free" is entirely accurate.

Being your true, authentic self may be simple—but it can also be challenging. Slowing down and being truthful goes against the "fake it 'til you make it" mentality that is the norm. The world tells us to go faster, "rise and grind," and "crush it" from the time we wake up until the time our head hits the pillow at night.

I'm interested in enjoying my life, and a rise-and-grind pace doesn't sound fun. I want to connect with people and make an impact. I know that will require work, and I will need traits like discipline and organization. But I'm interested in experiencing both success and joy at the same time. What's the use of success if you are miserable and exhausted?

Societal norms dictate that to look or sound cool, we have to do what the cool people do. Who writes these rules?

You won't look stupid by being truthful. In fact, the people who end up looking foolish are those who posture and pretend to know or be something they aren't.

That sounds complicated . . . and exhausting!

Truth is simple and, frankly, people are more alike than they are different. Most of us just want someone to care enough to dig a little and help us think better, love better, and be better.

Stop writing narratives based on assumptions.

Slow down and ask yourself what really needs to be accomplished today.

Ask people how you can help them.

Slow down and just *be*—one step and one day at a time.

LET'S GO WIN

"You'll never change your life until you change something you do daily. The secret of your success is found in your daily routine."

JOHN C. MAXWELL

Four

ROUTINES

An old friend recently came to visit. He and I went fishing for a few days and had an increrdible time. We reminisced about good times and also talked about the future.

After he went home, I felt zapped, almost like I had run a marathon. I felt undeniably off my game, and it took me nearly a week to get back into my usual mode of doing things.

I wouldn't change a thing about the visit and loved reconnecting, but it did get me thinking. As long as we stay the course and keep moving along the path, the wheels of progress remain in motion, too. The moment we veer off the trail, we feel an instant let down, like we've come off the rails.

This leads me to wonder: who is controlling whom? Do we control our daily routines, or do they control us?

That's a good question, but it's not one I'm able to answer fully. I can say, however, that every day, my goal is to give my all to whatever task or project I am doing, or to any person I am interacting with that day.

Do your best, every single day. Not someone else's best, but yours. You can accomplish this by consistently doing the things that make you your *very best.*

In other words, it's about finding a routine that sets you up to win.

When I was younger and played sports, like plenty of other athletes, I performed a particular routine before every game. Call it superstition if you want, but I simply recognized that when I did and said certain things before a game, I played well. When I didn't do those things, my performance would suffer.

What habits and routines make it simpler for you to win?

There is a lot of talk out there about forming good habits, and you may be wondering if *habit* and *routine* are the same things. The answer is yes, and no. Routines do consist of habits, but I prefer the word *routine* because it represents all of your best practices strung together.

Not to mention that the word *habit* can be limiting. That's the funny thing about language. Our brains become wired to judge particular words depending on how they are most often used. For many people, developing a new habit sounds intimidating. We used to be told that it takes 21 to 30 days to form a habit, but more recently, new research suggests that it takes 66 days.

Sounds tough, right? You could even interpret that to mean that if you work hard to develop a new habit for 53 days but then miss a day, all of that hard work was for nothing.

To make things a little more complicated, people tend to think of habits as things they need to break. Good habits can be easy to stop, while the bad ones are so easy to keep right on doing.

What about the word *routine* itself? Maybe to you, routines are boring but, in reality, it is the opposite. The kind of routine I'm talking about is a series of actions and mindsets that make you excited to take on the day—things that get you ready to bring your best to every aspect of life.

A routine *may* be predictable. But boring?

Never.

I coach on this idea more than any other. That's because when you have control over your routine, you will be victorious in your day, more easily find joy in life, and get more out of every effort and interaction.

START A PRACTICAL MORNING ROUTINE

Yes, the unexpected happens in life and things get in the way, but I still believe that for the most part, you get out of life exactly what you put into it.

With that idea in mind, I have designed a routine that maximizes each day's potential. It's my standard operating procedure for the first few minutes of every morning. When I take the time to perform each step, it puts me on the right path, and I feel ready to take on the world.

Everyone's routines will vary a little based on unique personality traits, home life, interests, bedtime, and wake-up time. In general, however, I have found a few things that should almost universally be a part of a powerful morning routine:

1. Get a full night's sleep.
I used to think four or five hours was enough sleep. I felt good and never thought twice about it. These days, I sleep eight hours a night,

thanks to a podcast I listened to about the irreversible brain damage that comes from not getting enough sleep. New research suggests that chronic lack of sleep could cause permanent damage to neurons, reduce your ability to pay attention, and lead to depression. I've also heard that the exact length of time required to do all the things our bodies must do during sleep varies, but I'm not taking any chances.

2. Work your brain.

After I wake in the morning, I continue my quest for a healthy brain by doing a few minutes of brain games. Alzheimer's and dementia terrify me, and this prompts me to give my mind a workout as regularly as possible. My training of choice is a brain exercise app called Lumosity, which takes about 15 minutes daily. If you have never done any sort of brain games, I highly recommend them! They are fun and beneficial.

3. Take time to meditate.

After my brain exercises, I meditate for five to ten minutes. My meditation time is certainly nothing fancy. I don't chant or cross my legs and ponder the nothingness of space and time. I simply find a quiet spot to breathe deeply and take stock of what comes floating across my mind. It is a few moments of clarity and peace in my day.

4. Fuel up with good stuff.

Next, I brew my morning coffee that includes a shot of MCT oil or "brain octane" healthy fats. This type of fat provides the body with a quick and healthy source of energy that helps get your cylinders firing and keeps them going. Donuts, bagels, and sugary lattes provide a brief jolt of energy soon followed by a crash. Find a source of fuel that keeps you full of energy and vitality.

5. Read a few pages.

Next, as I sip on my morning coffee, I read ten pages of a book. Most mornings, I end up reading more, but ten pages are my minimum. We become wired over time to think in specific, fixed ways. Reading helps feed us new ideas and provides us with different perspectives.

Some people excuse themselves from reading by saying, "I'm just not a reader." I'm not talking about reading a book a week. Just strive for ten pages or set a time limit such as ten minutes if that works better for you. If you are alive and have interests, there is bound to be a topic or an author that will resonate with you.

Years ago, my goal used to be one book a month. I found myself disappointed when I didn't reach that target. So, instead, I started reading ten pages each morning.

I don't care how busy you are—reading ten pages is not going to overwhelm anyone's day.

It doesn't have to be an actual book (an eBook or audiobook also works), but for me, the act of reading a physical book is essential. What we see has so much more influence over us than what we hear. Combine what you see with the sensation of turning the pages, and I find it has a profound impact on my brain and my sense of accomplishment.

6. Fit in some exercise.

When I exercise, I am a happier person, and I have so much more energy. I used to work out first thing in the morning, but since I prioritized sleep, I had to shift exercise to later in the day. If I have time before work, that's great. If not, I will stop by the gym, go for a walk with my wife, or play outside with my kids after work.

7. Practice active gratitude.

The thing about scientific studies—particularly the ones that give a specific number of days until something becomes a habit—is they tend to restrict us unintentionally. The number 66 is not magical. It's not like you will wake up on the 67th day and never have to consciously think about that habit again, as it has become a natural practice.

For some, good habits come quickly, and for others, they may require more effort and time. Several aspects of my routine took longer than a few months to internalize—and one of those was gratitude. For years I had been seeking to make gratitude an act that I practiced each day, even when I didn't feel particularly grateful.

Now that it has become part of my structure, I am working to instill the principle into my kids. When we sit down at the dinner table each evening to enjoy a meal together, I ask each of them, "What three things are you grateful for today?"

If one of my sons chooses Gatorade, pizza, and video games, I pass no judgment. I simply want to condition them to focus on the good in life.

If we focus on the good rather than on what we are lacking, our whole outlook changes. Instead of "Woe is me," it becomes, "Whoa, this is my life, and it's amazing!"

Don't live life as though you are stuck in the lyrics of a country song. Active gratitude is more of an action than a mindset, and you can absolutely work to make it an active part of your routine.

You get to decide what tone you set for each day.

The majority of average people wake up just in time to scramble out of bed and not be late to work. They don't take time to set the mood for the day. It doesn't have to be overwhelming or time-consuming. For most of us, there are a few "life hacks" that can help you perform at your peak.

Most people really don't want to trudge through life. If you're going to live life to its fullest, wake up to a routine that gets you excited about each new day.

REMINDERS BECOME HABITS, HABITS BECOME ROUTINES

The next part of my routine deserves its own section because it's a fundamental principle that I don't want you to miss. In addition to my other morning actions, I also read and recite the seven daily reminders that are posted on my bathroom mirror. These are the things I remind myself to focus on every single day, regardless of what I set out to accomplish:

1. *Have a growth mindset.* If something is hard at first, the default for many people is to give up. A growth mindset says, "This may be hard, but practice makes perfect." Decide to never give up!

2. *Be a leader at all times.* I realize this is relatively vague, but for me, it makes sense to be a leader at home and at work. This reminder helps hold me accountable for my actions.

3. *Take your ego out of it.* Ego only detracts, never adds. Ego gets in the way of honest, authentic connections and makes others feel excluded. Remove your ego and your need to always be right or the best in the room, and life will become exponentially easier.

4. *Be present in the now, fully engaged.* This one is really all-encompassing. My morning routine is what sets the tone for the day and brings me into the present. Then I remind myself, as often as necessary, to stay engaged and present in each moment—not full of regret about the past or worried about the future.

5. *Keep your perspective.* My beloved brother-in-law passed away in his late 40s from esophageal cancer. It hit our family like a ton of bricks, and it also put everything into perspective. Life is so fleeting. How big of a deal are those cold French fries, that flat tire, or the rush-hour traffic? If you are stuck in rush-hour traffic, remember that you are one of the lucky ones who has a car! If your kids are bouncing off the walls, think about the children who are dealing with chronic diseases or couples who are childless, despite years of trying. It's all about perspective.

6. *Your inner dialogue is a jerk. Be kind to yourself.* No one is harder on you than yourself. You are your worst critic. If the voices in your head are not lifting you up, tell them to be quiet.

7. *Be courageous, have fun, and transcend.* Courage helps us stay authentic. It keeps us from hiding behind our masks, and it also helps us stand up for what is right. And having fun ... what's the point without it? Always be ambitious, seek to go to the next level, and transcend.

Here's the really cool thing about this reminder list. My bathroom mirror used to have 13 daily reminders, but six of them have now become intrinsic habits (including read, meditate, be authentic, and focus on simplicity) and no longer need reminders.

I just get up and live them without thinking!

When a mindset or action becomes an intrinsic part of your routine, you take it down off the bathroom mirror. In this way, daily reminders become habits, which then become a natural part of your method of doing life.

The key is to focus on these reminders. Don't just put a sticky note on your computer and think that will be enough. Revisit them daily and think about ways to apply the principles to your life.

I encourage you to try this practice. Write down goals for daily life (not one-time tasks). Keep them posted until you internalize them. One day in the future, maybe 66 days from now, or maybe longer, you will realize you don't have to remind yourself to do a particular action or think a particular way. These goals and behaviors will have become automatic.

THE MODERN WORK-WEEK FALLACY

I've talked a lot about the morning and its critical role in your routine. But what about the rest of the day?

Is there a winning routine to use at work?

Before I answer that question, I'd like to ask you a question: Do you really need to work eight to ten hours a day, five days a week?

For some people, the answer may be "absolutely." But for a growing number of salaried employees, the answer is "absolutely not."

What if you're able to get all of your work done—and do it all well—in 25 or 30 hours? Daniel Pink talks about this in his book, *Drive*. Pink presents the idea of a "Results-Only Work Environment," where you are paid for results rather than time.

It makes so much sense, and yet far too few companies practice it. Requiring someone to sit at their desk for 40 hours regardless of whether their work is already done is ridiculous. It's like back in school when you were required to write a thousand-word essay but could have more succinctly written everything in 500 words. Instead, you had to invent another 500 words of fluff or else lose points.

Maybe you think long hours are required, but I believe we only work longer hours because we don't bring 100 percent of our effort and energy to the task in front of us. Someone once told me that: "It's not the hours you put into your work that matters, it's the work you put into the hours."

That's the beauty of becoming a better version of yourself by creating a winning routine. If you take the time in the morning to focus and get ready for the day and whatever it brings, I believe you will be able to work fewer hours while accomplishing more.

Why would you work in a distracted, fragmented manner for 12 hours when you could bring it all to the table for six hours, and then go home and hang out with your family?

Regardless of your type of workplace—whether you have to clock in and out or have a little bit more freedom—it's essential to be territorial with your time. For example, if you set aside time to get a particular project done, do not allow a phone call or email to distract you from the task at hand.

It's about giving everything you have to the thing or person in front of you.

In his book, *Smarter Faster Better*, Charles Duhigg talks about how much time we misuse at work. We don't set out to waste time—we are simply not protective enough of it. We sit down and decide to work on a specific task for the next half hour, but then the phone rings or a notification pops up on your phone. Before you know it, three hours have gone by, and you are no closer to completing that task.

To stop wasting time, you need three things:

1. A strong morning routine.

2. Full commitment to the thing or person in front of you.

3. Your trigger.

Let's talk about that last one for a minute. As a leader, as a parent, as an employee, or just as a human being, some situations require an extra boost. It could be before a game, a presentation at work, a romantic date, or a job interview.

In those moments, you have to bring it all and hold nothing back—and what you may need is a trigger to push you that extra inch into your most excellent state.

Music is definitely my trigger. I have a playlist of songs that pump me up and increase my energy the moment I hear them. For others, it could be saying a prayer, reading a quote, or doing pushups. Author and life coach Tony Robbins calls it your "power move."

So, if you want to win at work, start by finding the right morning routine. Decide to compartmentalize your tasks rather than multitask. Use your trigger to get in the zone and feel your brain come alive—and then give it everything you have. You'll get more out of the day in fewer hours. The consequence? You get to spend more time with the people you love or do the things you love.

CUT YOURSELF SOME SLACK

I've been meditating on and off for years, with far too much time spent in the "off" mode. The past four years, however, it has become consistent. I rarely miss a day.

Want to know what changed? I edited my meditation goal from "meditate 20 minutes a day" to "meditate daily." It finally stuck because I stopped putting a judgment on how long I did it. In the past, I would think, "If I'm not getting at least 20 minutes, I won't even bother." Now, if I meditate for 30 seconds one day, that's still a win.

An instrumental part of the whole message of vulnerability and simplicity is cutting yourself some slack. We're really hard on ourselves as a society. Women feel compelled to look a certain way thanks to a set of unrealistic standards, and men are fed the lie that to be "real men" they can't cry and must stay in perpetual "beast mode."

In college, I used to work out for two hours a day. Today, I'm lucky if I have 30 minutes to spare. Not to mention, I'm not as strong as I was back then. My default is to think, "What's the use? I'll never be in that kind of shape again!"

This kind of thinking is what compels a lot of people to shut down and give up altogether. I invite you to start cutting yourself some slack.

Life changes and your idea of success should change along with it.

Let your brain know it's okay not to hold yourself to the standard you applied when you were 21. When you use unrealistic benchmarks, you will end up disappointed every time.

Start small and keep going. Darren Hardy, the publisher of *SUCCESS Magazine*, teaches about the power of small but consistent effort in his book, *The Compound Effect*. Tiny steps and choices may seem insignificant at the moment, but over time, they amount to substantial changes.

Nobody likes to feel overwhelmed. When you try something new or attempt to develop a new habit, the challenge has the tendency to overwhelm or intimidate. If you are not used to reading, start with just two pages. That's it! If you are out of shape, go up and down the stairs at home one extra time, use the stairs instead of the elevator at work, or park your car further away and walk a few hundred feet to work.

Baby steps can change the world if they are taken consistently.

A successful workout could be stretching for ten minutes. Ten minutes is better than zero minutes, isn't it? The same thing goes for adjusting the time you go to bed or wake up. Go to bed half an hour earlier tonight and wake up 30 minutes sooner. In that extra half an hour you have in the morning, you can read, meditate, stretch, and get ready to rock the day.

If it helps, just set simple goals like "read" and "workout." That could amount to reading the first page of a new book and taking the stairs. The sense of accomplishment from completing a task is worth it. The amount of time you spend on that activity will naturally increase once you realize there is a point to it and notice the difference it makes.

Everybody should have a different definition of success that makes sense for their lives and what they value. So, first, figure out what success looks like for you, and then base your routines around that. If you have incredibly ambitious goals, that's great. But don't beat yourself up if you don't meet them.

As a fellow human being, what are you trying to accomplish today? My big, undeniable, overarching goal is simple (and I have a feeling yours is the same). When you break it down, most of us just want to be happy. We're not on Earth for long, so let's strive to make our time here as full of joy as possible.

If doing yoga makes you happy, do it. If you despise yoga, don't do it. If you can't read or meditate for a full 30 minutes, is someone going to send you to detention?

Who is going to beat you up over these things besides you?

Things don't have to look or feel like they did 20 years ago, or even five years ago. If you have a job, a family and friends, you are going to be naturally busy—and that's okay! The key is to find a routine that works for you and, perhaps more importantly, is sustainable.

Set a routine that enables you to consistently accomplish your goals and feel joy, each and every day.

LET'S GO WIN

"Intention is one
with cause and effect.
Intention determines
outcome. And if you
are stuck and not moving
forward, you have to
check the thought and
action that created
the circumstance."

OPRAH WINFREY

Five

INTENTION

Did you know that before the industrial revolution, the word *priorities* (with an *s*) didn't exist? There was just *priority*, which was the one most important thing (with no *s*) you had to do in a day.

After the industrial revolution, managers realized they could get more out of people if they gave them more than one priority. We've now evolved into a society where people have *dozens* of daily priorities . . .

And they are all of equal importance.

That makes no sense. Yet we live it every day! We prioritize one little item over another. In the end, we have a list of 167 things that all need to be done today.

That's an insane way to go about our lives. Where is the purpose in that? I don't know about you, but when my day becomes a flurry of activity and noise, the end result is I've done a bunch of things half-way.

The lack of clear intention is responsible for most of the adverse or disappointing outcomes we experience, which is why *being intentional* is the solution for turning mediocre performance, relationships, and results, into exceptional ones.

With so many distractions in this world, it's incredibly easy to stay busy all day long and end up accomplishing very little. However, when you act with intention, you have a clear purpose in mind for doing what you are doing, and the result is a day filled with genuine achievement.

Let's say you have 30 minutes to spend with the kids before dinner. If your goal is to check "play with kids" off your list, then maybe this doesn't apply to you. However, if your purpose is to make a lasting, positive impression on your children, you can decide to commit *all of you* during those 30 minutes. In fact, giving your kids half an hour of your undivided attention is far more meaningful than spending two hours with them while you simultaneously watch sports and check your phone.

When you act with intention, you give all of your focus and energy to a singular task or person. You'll find that once you give everything you have to one thing, you'll get better results and end up spending less time overall on daily tasks.

Consider it a life hack for getting more fulfillment and results out of life.

THE MULTITASK TRAP

The concept of giving 100 percent of yourself to one task at a time is in direct contrast to the concept of multitasking. As you might guess, I do not believe multitasking is the best way to achieve the most during any day.

There is a commonly held idea that women are better at multitasking than men. While there isn't any reliable empirical data to back up the idea that women are superior multitaskers, let's assume for the sake of argument that this is true.

Just because you may be good at something doesn't mean you are adopting the best approach. Try to juggle ten things at once, and one or more of those things *will* get dropped. Regardless of how skilled you may be at doing many things at once, it's still a more stressful way to live.

The intentional approach to undertaking tasks is uncomplicated and assures that each activity, person, or project gets your full attention. Why give 10 percent to ten things simultaneously, when you can give 100 percent to one individual thing, one at a time?

When people slow down and address one task before moving on to the next, they report greater efficiency and higher overall quality of work. The added benefit of this is that it helps reduce the sense of panic or constant stress that has become the *modus operandi* for many people.

From a biological standpoint, living in a state of constant stress and pressure causes the body to remain in "fight or flight" mode, which then causes us to react even more emotionally and harms the body's ability to operate in its optimal state.

Rather than laundry-listing every last bit of minutiae you *think* you need to do, stop and ask the question, "What am I trying to accomplish today?" Act with intention by asking yourself how to best use your time in the present moment.

Then do that task and do it well.

DECLARE YOUR PURPOSE

Intention is all about purpose and clarity. It's also one of the keys to effectively communicating with others (which we will talk about in more detail in a later chapter).

When you don't have a clear purpose for a conversation with your spouse, an email, or a meeting, it is painfully evident to the other person.

It's just as harmful to have a purpose but not share it.

No one should ever have to wonder what it is you're trying to say or accomplish. People universally respond favorably to direction and clarity, so give them what they want and need.

With all the distractions of life, it's hard enough to get your message across. So, take the time to slow down and state the *why*. Let people know that this is not just another meeting, another phone call, or a pointless conversation.

It should either be to serve an essential purpose, or why have it at all?

The right intention, communicated promptly, can help ensure the message is well received. Let's say you need to deliver some helpful critique to a struggling employee. There are three basic ways to approach this:

1. *Be overly critical and shame them into better performance.* This method leads to nothing but resentment and eventual failure.

2. *Side-step the issue and allow it to continue unchecked.* This may seem easier, but the problem will only intensify.

3. **Say what you mean.** Let the employee know you
   sincerely want to help them. Ask them if they want help,
   and then work together to find a solution. If someone
   says to you, "My intent is to help you," you will naturally
   be more open to hearing what they have to say.

If you want a message to be received appropriately, take the time to explain the purpose. That takes some additional effort but, in the long run, it will save you a lot of time and energy.

This intention also applies to you and your efforts to self-examine. Before you set a meeting or offer critique, ask internal questions like, "Am I only doing this because I'm angry?" or "Would I engage in this same conversation tomorrow?" or "Why am I really bringing this up?"

Ask yourself *why*, and you may just find your reasons are not compelling enough to continue with that activity.

This truly applies to every area of life.

Let's look at vacations. If you've ever traveled with young kids, you know that a family vacation is not particularly restful.

You could stop going on vacation. Or, what if you decide to create a purpose for the vacation that makes your efforts worthwhile? Decide to enjoy the trip and don't put pressure on yourself to force relaxation or—at the other end of the spectrum—force activity for the sake of activity.

Don't live and die by the itinerary. If you can't fit in all the activities, who cares? Is everyone (including mom and dad) having fun? Set out to have fun and stop when it's no longer fun.

When I ask about people's vacations, I often hear the same response. "I need a vacation to recover from the vacation [insert eye roll]. It was so exhausting!"

What if your purpose was to have fun, not to relax; to see new things and share new experiences with your family? What if your vacation doesn't look like the pictures of your friends' vacations on Facebook? That's all a façade anyway.

Be purposeful and decide to go on vacation for the right reasons, and the trip will be what you make of it.

Does your daily schedule have purpose? If your schedule is over-committed, and you are feeling like a bag floating in the wind, go back to intention. Ask yourself questions like:

- Why do I have this on my calendar?
- Does my child enjoy this activity?
- Do I enjoy this activity?
- Can we afford to do this?
- Would we miss this if it were out of our lives?
- Does this take up too much of our quality family time?

If your purpose is to become a human taxi and your intention is "to involve my kids in as many activities as possible," then that type of schedule may work for you.

But have you ever thought about whether it fits your children's intentions?

One possible way to whittle down the schedule is to *ask* your kids what they want! My oldest son wants to pursue tennis, and so we spend most of his free time on that one activity. My youngest son goes back and forth on his tastes and preferences. When he starts to balk at going to football practice, we don't guilt him into going by saying the famed parental line, "I paid for this, and you committed to it, so you're going!"

Instead, we say, "Okay, let's revisit why you wanted to do this in the first place."

The point is to bring him back to his original intent and purpose for playing the sport. This approach is very well received and almost always works to fire him back up again. He just needs from time to time to be reminded of his intention!

Forcing your kids or an employee to do something without clearly establishing the purpose will quickly become a lesson in futility and frustration.

Let's stop imposing what we think is best and instead open up honest dialogue about intentions.

DON'T LIVE BY ACCIDENT

When it comes to parenting, my wife prefers a structured approach to the day. Our boys adhere to a plan that she has determined is the best for them. Meals, school, practices, bedtime, and play dates all operate on a set agenda.

This is a common scenario for plenty of families, and that's because parenting, work, marriage, and more—each of the most prominent areas of our lives is ruled by routine.

The question, then, is not *if* a routine will be a part of your life, but *what kind* of routine is best? Is it one that runs on reactive decisions and habitual frantic activity, or is it an intentional one that is designed to accomplish specific goals?

Intention is not something you will ever be able to put onto autopilot. In fact, intention at its core is an *act*—a physical, mental, and even emotional decision.

Creating the right habits and routines must be intentional. However, even when you plan out the most perfect day, life can still get in the way. Flat tire, sick kids, unexpected work crisis. These things happen —and they happen to everyone. You are not the lone exception.

So, how do you bounce back?

By being intentional.

I have learned the hard way that you don't get more done by speeding up.

You get more done by slowing down.

When the day seems to be getting away from you, don't run to try to catch up. Instead, stop and regroup. You have the choice to lead a reactive lifestyle or a proactive one that is driven by intention.

I am clear on my daily goals and what needs to be done, but I also know that when unexpected things happen, I may have to stop and reassess.

This type of behavior won't happen overnight. It's going to take practice. It's also going to require a concerted effort to be crystal clear about what you are doing and why.

Being intentional leads to fulfillment. It feels so good to have set out to accomplish something and then get it done—and done well. No more making scatterbrained mistakes or forgetting what you were doing while in the middle of the task.

Our days on Earth are numbered. To me, one of the worst feelings in the world is going to bed at night knowing I squandered one of my precious days by not being intentional.

I want to make sure that I make each day count, and I encourage you to do the same.

"Do what you
say you're going to do.
And try to do it
a little bit better than
you said you would."

JIMMY DEAN

· Six ·

ACCOUNTABILITY

My parents did their best to impart pearls of wisdom to me when I was young. Most of it went in one ear and out the other. One particular insight, however, I was unable to ignore. For as long as I can remember, my parents told me time and time again, "Son, just do what you say you're going to do."

It was a profound but straightforward lesson. My parents are firm believers in being held accountable for your words and actions. When you are accountable, it means you take responsibility for the things to which you have committed that either happened or didn't happen.

Your word is your bond. Your word is also precious and valuable—and once people lose faith in what comes out of your mouth, you will have to work extremely hard to earn their confidence again.

In some cases, you may never get it back.

If you want to consider just how potent the word "accountable" is, try this quick exercise: Draw a line down the center of a blank piece of paper. At the top left, write "accountable" and on the other side, write "victim." Next, write down all the attributes associated with each.

For example, under accountable, you may write words like responsible, acceptance, maturity, and understanding. Under the victim side, you might choose words like scared, helpless, complaining, and passive.

You will quickly notice that on the accountability side, the vast majority of the attributes are empowering, while on the victim side, most are negative. There may be a few positive traits like empathy or sympathy on the victim side, but for the most part, accountability is empowering, while being a victim is debilitating.

In short, having a victim mentality is the polar opposite of holding yourself accountable for your words and actions.

DON'T PLAY THE VICTIM CARD

At its core, accountability comes down to one word: Blame.

For those with a victim mentality, the blame always rests on someone else's shoulders. For those who are accountable for their words and actions, however, there is no pointing of fingers.

From time to time, we all fail to keep our word. This is human and to be expected. There are also times when it really is someone else's fault.

However, if you have let someone down—even if it is through no fault of your own—the last thing anyone wants to hear is you blaming it on someone else or on circumstances that were beyond your control.

People don't care who messed it up or why. They just want you to do what you say you are going to do.

If you don't, then they expect you to make it right without hesitation.

In a collaborative, results-only work environment, the reasons something wasn't accomplished really don't matter. Don't hide behind an excuse. Instead, step forward and just get things done.

I recently hired a contractor for a backyard project, and I quickly discovered that he was a card-carrying member of the victim's club. It was always someone else's fault when he missed a deadline. All I ever wanted to hear him say was, "I'm sorry. This won't happen again, and I'll do our best to make it right."

Not once did he assume accountability for the progress of the project.

In the end, the work got done, but now, instead of giving glowing reports to my friends about him, I have advised everyone I know to steer clear of him and his company.

Don't be that person who others talk about with an avoid-at-all-costs warning.

The heart of the issue boils down to trust. If you say you're going to do something, but then you don't do it and then blame someone else, trust begins to erode. If you fail to keep your word and shift the blame, all confidence slowly fades away—and so does the chance of a good relationship.

No one wants to hear your excuses, no matter how good or valid you think they are. When you say you will do something, but it doesn't happen, take responsibility.

Then fix it.

HAVE REALISTIC EXPECTATIONS

If you want to prevent that sinking feeling of having to apologize for not coming through on a commitment, I highly recommend under-promising and over-delivering.

Don't wear the overachiever's mask if you can't live up to the hype. When you promise more than you can pull off, your flippant "sure, no problem" attitude ends up *being* the problem.

Simply don't set expectations you can't match.

We all know people who are professional talkers. They say what they think we need to hear—but they never live up to their own hype. After a while, we learn we can't trust a thing that comes out of their mouth.

The only results that come from giving false or inflated promises are disappointment and resentment. This then creates long-lasting and pervasive trust issues. You begin to think, "If this person lies about small things, what else are they lying about?

If you are prone to promising the moon but failing to deliver, it's time to come back down to earth and start being realistic. With time and intention, you can rebuild trust. However, the real and possibly irreparable damage is done when you let someone down repeatedly, and the damage is even more severe when you play the victim card.

In such cases, trust has eroded and will likely never be regained—and that's because the tendency to be unreliable and pass the buck is indicative of a more serious underlying problem:

Being prone to dishonesty.

I can deal with pretty much everything except lying. Fool me once, and I'll cut you a break. But (and maybe it's because I'm a baseball fan) it's three strikes, and you're out.

An established pattern of lying is not something that can be overlooked. Chronic failure to keep one's word is a severe character flaw. We all have bad days, bad weeks, or even bad months. But at some point, you either stand by your word, or you reveal that this is just how you are.

TAKE EXTREME OWNERSHIP

Each one of us will fail during our lives. Sometimes, there will be legitimate reasons, and other times there won't. However, it's not really about the *reasons*—it's about the *response*.

The most impressive thing you can do is take ownership, both when it is your fault, and *especially* when it's not your fault.

It can be frustrating to be blamed for something that happened outside our realm of control. Maybe it's pride, ego, or a personal standard of excellence, but something in us wants others to know, "But this really wasn't my fault!"

As natural as the tendency may be to want others to know you are not to blame, I encourage you to try a different approach. When you are involved with a project or task that goes wrong through no fault of your own, take complete responsibility for it.

Don't offer excuses.

Just own it.

All of it.

There's a book by Jocko Willink and Leif Babin called *Extreme Ownership: How the U.S. Navy Seals Lead and Win* that speaks to this point. It makes it clear that on the field of battle, it's life and death every day. If a fellow soldier is killed, no excuses can bring that friend back. Someone may or may not have done their job correctly, but does it really matter? What matters is owning the mistake as a unit and doing your best to ensure it doesn't ever happen again.

You should take ultimate responsibility, no matter how much of a role you played in any failure.

This type of attitude not only fosters team spirit, but it's also incredibly inspiring to those around you. The next time something goes wrong, or a deadline is missed, remember this four-letter acronym that encapsulates how to take ownership:

Summarize what happened.

Explain the result.

Apologize without shifting blame.

Let them know how you will make it right.

We bend over backward to work with people and companies who take ownership. Nordstrom and Amazon have both built radical, unwavering loyalty thanks to their willingness to take ownership and never shift the blame to their customers.

If a company gives every excuse in the world why it's not their fault and offers no solution to make it better, they don't deserve my business. The same goes for the people in my life. If someone is not willing to be responsible for their actions, they don't deserve to have a relationship with me.

Words don't mean a whole lot if your actions don't back them up. In the battle between what you say and what you do, what you do wins every time in terms of proving your character. Some people talk a good game and never follow up. As the famous unattributed quote says, "Words are meaningless without intent and follow-through."

My general observation is that the loudest person in the room generally has the least amount of follow-through. One exception to this is Muhammad Ali. Ali was a big talker who was full of bravado and bold claims. The amazing and unusual thing is he always lived up to his own hype. He was an outlandish showman, but no one could deny that he was a man of his word.

In general, however, the "small dogs" of the world tend to bark the loudest. Of course, I don't mean physically small, but small in the sense that they are not men or women of their word and are generally all façade and no substance.

The "big dogs," on the other hand, are the strong men and women who are slower to speak and more prone to getting things done without excuses. We trust these "St. Bernards" of the world. They rescue Timmy and don't brag about it. They just get it done and get back to work.

STEPS TO BECOMING ACCOUNTABLE

I stumbled across this anonymous quote about accountability, and it really sums everything up perfectly: "Personal accountability requires mindfulness, acceptance, honesty, and courage."

There will always be circumstances outside of your control. You can either complain about them or accept them.

You may think you've been dealt more than your fair share of adversity and have earned the right to play your victim card. Oprah Winfrey experienced tremendous hardship in her youth. I doubt anyone would have thought twice if she stayed in the shadows and remained a victim her entire life.

As we know, that's not what happened.

She didn't let circumstances that were beyond her control dictate her life or define her.

What has happened to you in life may not be your fault. However, the way you allow those events to shape you is undoubtedly up to you.

Take full responsibility for your life, and in this way, instead of life happening *to* you, life can start happening *for* you.

Maybe you have struggled with keeping your word. You can fix that. It's really never too late, so here are my four simple steps to becoming more accountable in your life:

1. Write it down.

From the big goals to the daily chores, writing down your responsibilities is proven to be effective. Take that a step further by placing those words where you can see them daily. I put my biggest goals on my bathroom mirror so I will see them at least two times a day. I have heard that New Year's resolutions are 80 percent more likely to be kept when they are written down. Life throws endless distractions our way. Don't force your brain to remember everything. Just write it down.

2. Don't overcommit.

Keep promises realistic and straightforward. If you can't finish a task by a specific date, don't say you can and expect forgiveness when you fail.

3. Give others permission to hold you accountable.

Freely empower others to hold you accountable. Give your spouse and co-workers permission to hold you to your word by saying, "Please call me out on this if I don't do what I say." When you give somebody permission to hold you accountable, then whatever advice they provide on the topic is no longer unsolicited (and therefore more positively received). Tell people, "I want to get better. So, please hold me accountable."

4. Inspect what you expect.

Billionaire investor, hedge fund manager, and philanthropist Ray Dalio talks about the importance of "radical transparency" in his *New York Times* bestselling book, *Principles*. In his business, after every significant meeting, they do a critique of what went right and what areas may need improvement. How liberating would it be to be able to point it out when you see something wrong? It's truly a game changer.

You get a fresh opportunity every day to do things a little bit better than you did the day before. Your partner, your kids, your friends, and your co-workers deserve for you to keep your word.

I don't know anyone who enjoys letting people down by not keeping their word. Your word is the only thing that you have over which you have complete control—and you have a chance to honor it or screw it up.

When you do screw up, own it.

We should all be trying to put ourselves in a position to win. Let other people help you become more accountable and help them in return.

"In today's rush,
we all think too much,
seek too much,
want too much,
and forget about the
joy of just being."
ECKHART TOLLE

· Seven ·

MINDFULNESS

My mouth has at times been known to move faster than my brain.

We've all been there. We hastily and carelessly react to something that someone says or does, and we either instantly regret it, or regret it once we have had more time to think.

It's the hallmark of every heated debate between husbands and wives since the beginning of time. If they had kept better records during the Stone Age, I do not doubt that somewhere in the chronicles of history, we would have read about a cave husband who told his cave wife that her dodo bird stew was the worst and, in retaliation, she called him a lousy spear maker.

This couple had real problems to deal with: saber-toothed tigers, starvation, freezing to death. But words can hurt, too, can't they?

So often we say and do things without thinking. We carelessly label others. We interrupt. We juggle tasks better than circus clowns. We are busy, inconsiderate, selfish, and just . . . ruffled.

The solution to stop the madness is *mindfulness*.

Some people associate mindfulness with yoga or new-age practices, but for me, it's far more practical and valuable. Being mindful begins internally, but it also has a lot to do with your words—their intention, their meaning. It also has to do with how you interpret the words and actions of others. Perhaps, even more so, it has to do with the words you choose *not* to say.

There is one comparison that cuts right to the heart of mindfulness, and that is: *respond versus react*. When you are mindful, you don't *react* to things. You *respond* to them. You decide that you will have dominion over the present moment and not be guilty of letting life slip by unnoticed, making snap judgments, or allowing unchecked words to escape your lips.

THE GATEWAY TO MINDFULNESS

There's a certain spiritual aspect to mindfulness. Whether that spirituality comes through worship, connecting with nature, or finding an activity that connects our heart to our actions, we all have something that grounds us.

What does it mean to be grounded? It means you slow down and respond to the day. You don't go 90 miles an hour from the moment you climb out of bed. It's about being deliberate and appreciative.

Nothing helps me be grounded more than meditation. It has held a valuable place in my life for 20 years, and over the last four years, it's become a part of my daily routine. I don't function well without it, because it's my gateway to mindfulness.

When I meditate, I am far less likely to have one of those days that "just got away from me." When I meditate, I value life and all that I have.

Over the past few decades, people have become increasingly interested in mindfulness meditation. Because of the growing interest, more and more clinical studies are being conducted to research the many benefits of meditation. There used to be just a handful of trials proving a vast array of positive effects (both physical and mental), but now, there are thousands.

We are starting to understand that in this world full of distractions and noise, we need a few moments of mindful meditation every day.

In fact, we need it desperately.

From tuning in to the news and scrolling away on our phones to overcommitting and multitasking, there is no shortage of ways to become distracted and detached from the here and now.

Ralph Waldo Emerson wrote, "I wish that life should not be cheap, but sacred. I wish the days to be as centuries, loaded, fragrant." I love the idea of living a "fragrant" life, but we don't stop and smell the roses anymore. Instead, we trample the roses and keep running.

Unless you are Usain Bolt, when is speed ever the right pace? What do you tell kids at the pool? Slow down and don't run! What do you do in traffic when it's raining and you want to avoid an accident? You drive more slowly and deliberately. What do you do when you want to phrase an email or a letter just right and make the best impression? You write slowly and choose your words carefully. What do you do when you are speaking to a group and want them to understand your message? You speak slowly and carefully.

Everything that we do well, we do deliberately and intentionally.

Yet, here we are, scurrying through life at breakneck speed.

Not only are we distracted by what we are doing, but we are also preoccupied with what we have already done or still need to do. We get stuck peering into the past or looking into the future, when the truth is, as Eckhart Tolle wrote in his book *The Power of Now*, nothing else matters except this precise moment.

Being mindful helps you understand this and to become intentional, with a focus on the present moment. If you want an even more straightforward way to remember that, here it is:

Being mindful is about being present in the present.

MINDFULNESS IS SELFLESSNESS

When you're at work, is your mind at the beach? When you're at the beach, is your mind at work? When you're playing with the kids, are you watching your favorite team or scrolling through Facebook as well?

When you're engaged in any conversation or activity, all of you should be there if your goal is to *achieve* in life and not just *endure* it.

We have interactions and conversations every day where we are not fully present. We might as well be holograms. It seems we have lost the ability to show up, slow down, and listen.

Instead of listening, most people are thinking more about what they want to say, and just waiting for their turn to talk.

We all want to be heard—and we all *deserve* to be heard. But there is a constructive way to be heard and a destructive way.

The first thing you must decide is if you are willing to communicate with selflessness. When two people are speaking, there is a good chance that one person will do more talking than the other. I make it my goal to be the listener. If I leave a conversation having listened far more than I have spoken, I consider that to be an unqualified success.

Maybe you think, "But I have important things to say, too!" As I said, we all deserve to be heard. But mindfulness comes from recognizing when it is your time to speak and when others will be better served when you listen.

Serving others is no easy task, but it does become more comfortable with practice. When you strive to be mindful, one of the most surprising and refreshing things you'll discover is that there are far fewer things that even *need* to be said, and the need to talk for the sake of talking fades.

The sound of your voice will no longer serve to fill some acceptance void because the void will no longer exist.

If you don't love the idea of always being the listener and never the star of the conversation, you are not alone. There are a few select people in my life who genuinely care about what I have to say. How do I know? Because they ask me questions!

They also listen without me compelling them or expecting them to listen.

So, listen and be genuinely interested in others. Then, when you do find *your* tribe of people, they will do the same for you.

In those relationships, everyone gets to share the spotlight. That's when talking about your children or your work promotion doesn't come off as bragging. It's more like a celebration of each other's lives and successes.

Mindfulness is about being selfless because, the truth is, most people are hurting, and they genuinely need you. There is always someone who is going through a trial that is harder than yours. I guarantee it. You can help shine a little more light into the world by closing your mouth and opening your ears and your heart.

When you are present in the present and approach interactions mindfully, your ego is less likely to drive the conversation. You can't be mindful and egotistical at the same time. The two things cannot co-exist.

However, there's not much you can do about the ego of others. There is no doubt that plenty of people love to talk about themselves—and if these types of people bother you, you are not alone.

Just remember that ego and insecurity go hand in hand. The most boastful men and women I know are also in the most pain. They are desperately trying to fill an unfillable well.

Let people say what they need to say. If you listen closely enough, you may break through to the real version of them and make a connection —and possibly even help them begin to heal.

LABELS BLOCK MINDFULNESS

It's hard not to use labels. We all do it, and it happens in the blink of an eye. Sometimes we label a person before we even speak to them based on their job, reputation, car, hairstyle, accent, or virtually any-thing else.

Maybe it's the way they chew their gum. Perhaps you don't like the way they laugh. There is no limit to the extent of our shallowness, and there's almost nothing we won't use to label. Then we neatly file that folder away and conclude we know all about that person.

If you want to live a mindful life, the labels must go.

When I enter into any new conversation, I resolve to do two things. First, I go in with a clean slate. Second, I go in intending to genuinely connect, not planning to gut through a superficial conversation with someone who I think I've got all figured out because of where they're from, what they look like, or what they do for a living.

When you resolve to become mindful, you are far less prone to make snap judgments. Our labels are rarely accurate anyway, so why bother? I say we replace labels with curiosity. Here is how that might sound:

I meet John, and thanks to some mutual acquaintances, I already know he has a reputation for being an egomaniac who loves to talk about himself. When I meet him, he seems to be living up to his reputation. Plenty of false bravado. No questions. It's all about John. It's like I tuned into the "John is Awesome" channel, and now the remote is broken.

There is a decision to make. I could either conclude, "John is precisely what everybody says he is," or I could choose to become curious. I pick curious, so I say, "Hey John, I've already heard these amazing things about you from our mutual friends. Tell me something no one else knows about you."

I guarantee you this will catch John off guard. At that moment, you'll see his defenses come down. It may go right back up, and he may not divulge much, but what if he did? What if you found out that John overcame a severe illness when he was a baby, or maybe that he secretly watches cooking shows in the hopes of being a chef one day?

John says the things he thinks will make him fit in and be an accepted member of society. Instead, you can invite him to stand out. Chances are his heart will jump at the opportunity to be seen in a real way.

I'm not suggesting this is easy. You may not even believe it's possible for egomaniacs like John to be vulnerable. However, that's not mindfulness talking. Be open, because you never know.

If John does choose to engage, your night just went from agonizing to interesting. I'd say that's a win! If he doesn't participate, you know you gave it your best effort and approached the conversation free from judgment. That's also a win.

Don't label the Johns of this world and, while you're at it, stop labeling yourself. Labels are just social constructs. We place ourselves into tiny boxes all the time.

"Hi, I'm David, and I'm a teacher."

"Hi, I'm Susan, and I'm an accountant."

That is not who David and Susan are. That is what they do to earn a living.

We are programmed to introduce ourselves with our pre-defined label(s) attached, but who says you have to keep following the herd? The next time you introduce yourself, I want you to try something new. I want you to lead with your "I Believe" statement.

Let's say someone introduces himself or herself with the typical greeting of name, job title, and company. When it's your turn, go beyond
the typical intro, using this as the template:

"I believe that . . . That is why I help . . . The goal is to . . ."

Here is how that might sound for Greg, who does financial planning
for young executives:

"I believe that *every person deserves to feel financially secure and con-*
fident about their future, no matter their age or current earning potential.
That is why I help *young professionals plan for their retirement*
long before most advisors would even consider working with them. **The**
goal is *to give them the freedom to pursue their real dreams rather than*
live in fear or worry."

That would make quite the impression; most certainly, the logical progression is your listener would be intrigued and probably ask more
questions that get to the heart of what matters, rather than continue
with questions that don't add much value, such as, "So, how long have
you worked there?"

They say that more work is done on a golf course than in a board-
room. The reason is because people connect on a whole different level
when they aren't wearing their labels. It's not, "I'm James, the businessman." Instead, it becomes, "I'm James, the guy who wants to help
people, who likes to fish, and who loves being a dad."

Labels are limiting and inaccurate. I promise you that I am not the
same person I was back in college, five years ago, or even last week.

We are all continuously morphing and evolving.

I regularly hear people say things like, "I'm just not a reader." What's true is that maybe you read a couple of books a few years ago that were boring, and you lost your excitement for reading. Don't limit yourself like this. Ask friends for book recommendations that helped shape their lives and try again.

The only label that ever sticks is "dead." I'm not ready for that one yet, so I am going to keep trying and pushing my limits. When I do, I almost always find that any labels I had were illusions rather than real limitations.

Be present without prejudice in the present moment; don't bring your own bias into your conversations, because that's not other people's problem. That's your problem.

It's easier to let someone talk while you silently judge them. That's a no-brainer. You could do that in your sleep. What's hard is digging in and keeping an open mind. Mindfulness requires you to remain fluid and ready to discover something new and unexpected.

COMMUNICATE WITH PURPOSE

If you struggle with remaining present in meetings, in conversations, or even at dinner with family, one question may help you stay mindful:

What do I want out of this?

What is the goal of your next meeting? What would the ideal outcome be for this conversation you are having with your boss? *Crucial Conversations* is a phenomenal book by four *New York Times* bestselling authors about how to get the most out of high-stakes interactions and critical moments in our lives.

Life-changing relationships can begin and end with one single conversation. The seeds of misunderstanding from one brief chat can grow into a forest of bitterness and resentment. Our interactions with other people in our lives are too significant to push to the backburner of our conscious minds.

If you are talking to someone, no matter how commonplace the conversation may seem, bring yourself into the present moment by thinking, "What do I want out of this conversation?"

I'm not talking about what you *think* you need to say or what you'd like the other person to say, but rather, what result do you want? Do you want to make a friend? Do you want this person to become a client? Perhaps you want to help a co-worker improve his or her performance?

Courage is like a muscle; it gets stronger the more we exercise it. At first, it is terrifying to approach interactions with such boldness and authenticity, but over time, it does get easier.

What do you want? A lot of the time, your goal and another person's goal may not be reciprocal. But if you have a purpose for the conversation, you will be more likely to hear their words and scan them for the real meaning rather than judge the entire interaction at face value.

Take full responsibility for your words and actions and assign a goal to them. Don't haphazardly wander through life. Even if you fail or a relationship collapses, you can say, "I gave it my best, but it wasn't meant to be." Regret is not something you ever want if you can avoid it.

MINDFULNESS REQUIRES A FILTER

You really can't change people's beliefs. As convenient as that would be, it's pretty hard to do. Debating with someone can actually serve to strengthen resolve on both sides.

So, does that mean it's pointless to talk with people who don't agree with you? Certainly not. I enjoy hearing what people have to say, and I go into conversations wanting to know more about their views.

I touch my heart frequently when I talk, and that is because when I speak with others, I sincerely try to connect my heart with theirs and remain open to what they're saying. I'm ready to ask questions—not so I can provide the best rebuttal, but so I can understand.

I've never shifted a person's most cherished beliefs. Not once. Why even try? State your truth and allow them to state theirs. Being mindful is about respect—and it requires being respectful of other's space, beliefs, opinions, goals, and priorities.

People love to judge what matters most to others. We think, "Well, that's not the way I would do it" or "I can't believe he likes that person."

Think about how much goes on inside your head that no one else knows. Guess what? Everyone has that same internal, hidden world. However, another part of mindfulness is knowing what should come out of that inner world and what should remain classified.

Let's say you are having a rough day. There's a good chance that without meaning to, you will bring those bad vibes into each conversation you have. Consequently, everyone with whom you interact now has your baggage to deal with, too.

If you want to be mindful of others, you need to check those attitudes and emotions.

I'm not knocking the importance of being truthful and authentic. However, it's essential to understand what other people are receiving from you. It's not about dishonesty. Our role as fellow human beings is to provide the ideal environment for others to be the best versions of themselves.

So, if you are having a bad day or have just received some terrible news, what can you do? Is there a way to control your communication without being fake or insincere?

I'm still a work in progress, but I've learned that it's possible to become more mindful of how your thoughts and feelings affect others. The first step is to be awake and aware of what your feelings are in the first place.

The next step is to approach each day with mindful intention so that you are ready to identify emotions as soon as you sense them. If you feel anger rising in your body, acknowledge it for what it is by saying to yourself, "This is what anger feels like for me."

If you are mindful of your emotions and identify some baggage that you should keep tucked away, ask yourself, "Would this feeling be valuable or harmful to others?"

If the answer is "harmful," then you need to find a trigger that will help you move past that feeling, so you don't bring others down.

Finding a trigger that helps improve your mood is an excellent way to keep all of your emotions from spilling out with no filter. My trigger is always music. Certain songs can bring a smile to my face no matter how dark the day has been.

Being mindful requires a filter because you don't want to give off negative energy. To combat the natural tendency to mirror those around you, find a trigger that can bring you back into the present moment. Remember, being positive helps others remain at their best.

SPEAK YOUR TRUTH AND EMBRACE THEIRS

Our brains are naturally wired to protect us and help us stand up for what's right and decent. However, that tendency is also what causes us to label others. The world needs less judgment and more caring— but we also shouldn't have to sit back and take what people dish out, regardless of how it makes us feel.

Recently, a salesperson was trying to sell me some expensive fitness equipment. I shared the same concern I had about durability with him three times, but he never even acknowledged what I said. We scheduled a follow-up call, and when he called me back, I could've easily told him, "I'm not interested," and hung up the phone.

But I didn't. Instead, I said, "I'm not interested, and here's why."

I told the salesperson that I didn't feel heard and that he had never bothered to address my real, stated concerns.

He was both floored and apologetic. Maybe it helped his future inter-actions with other customers, and maybe it didn't. But I left that con-versation knowing I had tried to help him treat others with a little more respect, and I didn't allow him to trample over me.

Speak your truth and give people room to speak theirs, and the result is you exist in a more authentic place. There is a motto I recite to my team regularly, which is:

"You may not always like me, but you can always trust me."

If you work with me, you may not like what I'm saying, but you can trust it. My words come from a place of love, not ego. I want what's best for the people around me.

That is the essence of being mindful.

If you want to be more mindful, start with meditation. No matter how you do it, find a grounding, peaceful way to awaken your feelings. It could be writing or reading poetry, going to church, taking a nature hike, or engaging in a form of meditation. There are plenty of meditation apps available for your smartphone that can guide you through the process if you are unsure of what to do.

Find something that allows you the space to slow down so that life doesn't go by without you ever awakening to all of its joy, connection, and beauty.

Meditation is just the jumping-off point, a way to get your day started with intention. The father of Western mindfulness, Jon Kabat-Zinn, said, "The real meditation is how you live your life."

Remember that your troubles are not the only problems in the world, and your successes are not the only ones that deserve to be celebrated. The spotlight is meant to be shared. Avoid labels and instead, communicate with purpose. You will get more out of every interaction if you become consciously aware of the why behind it.

If you want to change something, achieve a goal, build a new relationship, or mend an existing one, mindfully keep your eyes open all day long to what lies beneath the surface in the here and now.

"If you talk to a man
in a language
he understands,
that goes to his head.
If you talk to him
in his language,
that goes to his heart."
NELSON MANDELA

· *Eight* ·

COMMUNICATION

"Communication is everything."

A statement like this is another one of those everyday comments people hear that simply go in one ear and out the other.

From work to home to friendships, we all know that communication is vital in every area of life. We get it. But do we really?

In my experience, we often give communication lip service rather than intentional effort. It is one of those things we say we know all about, but we don't actively work to make improvements.

In the most literal sense of the word, *communication* is the transfer of information. We were not born with the power of telepathy. If we want one or more people to know something, we must transfer that knowledge to them. That's just how it works.

Unfortunately, that's where the simplicity stops. Honest communication that results in mutual understanding and correct interpretation is hard to accomplish without a plan and plenty of practice.

Even then, we're bound to get it wrong from time to time.

It's not a perfect science or art form, and there are virtually an endless number of ways to interpret a message—thanks to all of the biases we carry around with us.

There are many formally recognized biases, one of which is called *anchoring.* That is when you allow the first piece of information (for example, preconceived notions or negative first impressions) to cloud everything you receive after that. There is the *bandwagon effect,* also called groupthink, where you refuse to share a new or radical idea for fear of being viewed as a non-conformist. There's *optimism bias* and *pessimism bias.* And don't forget *status quo bias.*

We could go on for a long time and not list all the barriers to effective communication—and thanks to the conditioning we receive during our youth (watching our parents and friends communicate, cultural influences, platforms and technologies), there is no limit to the number of potential ways we could miscommunicate and misinterpret.

We don't speak our truth.

We misunderstand another person's intent.

We just plain don't listen.

I'm not bringing all of this up to make you feel hopeless. If anything, my goal is to let you know that you are not alone. We all want to be seen and heard, and yet we so often are not.

Honesty is tough. You are programmed to think you can't be honest. You'll hurt someone's feelings. People will think you are weird. So, you put on your mask, as does everyone else. It's a mess.

Instead of being honest, we mask the real message with fluff and fillers. Why do we do this? Again, that answer is complicated. However, the solution is simple:

The key to effective communication is not to tell people what you *think* they want to hear, but to speak truth. Be open and honest but also kind. When you do these things, you build trust, and that's when the real communication begins.

No mystery meanings. No passive-aggressiveness. Just real talk. In other words:

Say what you mean and mean what you say.

In this chapter, I'm not going to get technical or quote from a communication textbook. I'm going to speak from the heart, which is always the best way.

DETERMINE THE DESIRED OUTCOME

One of the foundational pieces of excellent communication goes back to several points already discussed. The first is *intention*. As an extension of that, effective communication requires answering the one question you must always ask yourself before engaging in any form of interaction:

"What do I want out of this?"

What results or outcomes would indicate that communication has been a success? These are not your selfish or personal emotional needs, but rather the ideal results for everyone involved.

It can be tough to place your own needs second, especially in personal relationships. If my wife and I are quarreling, I could easily let ego and pride stand in the way of effectively communicating. I've certainly done it before. She'll say something like, "You didn't do the dishes," and I'll shoot back with, "Well, you forgot to get me more toothpaste from the store."

I could do this. But why would I want to? How would that conversation go? If my goal is to make a big thing out of a little thing, I would be successful. However, that's never a goal—at least it shouldn't be.

Imagine instead what would happen if I shut my mouth and said, "Sorry about that. I'll do the dishes now."

What do I want out of the interaction? I love my wife, and I want a better relationship. I also want us to get past a minor issue and enjoy our evening.

Determining your purpose for communicating will give you a huge hand up in life. It will also clearly reveal which form of communication would be best to achieve the desired result.

If a message is absolutely critical, you should speak it, not write it. Face to face communication is best for significant issues. If it's a matter of the heart, don't even think about texting or emailing. Call or visit!

Although we could probably break them down further, there are four basic options for verbally communicating a message:

1. **Text:** Texting and messaging on social media apps should be used only for the most informal communications. We misinterpret texts with great ease, so keep texts casual and light.

2. **Email/Letter:** Email is one micro-level above texting. It is more socially acceptable for business. A letter is also

a more formal form of communication. However, if a message is crucial, skip the written word and try a phone call or in-person meeting.

3. **Phone:** On the phone, you can hear tone and voice inflection, and you can check for understanding, which is vital. It is, however, missing the critical element of nonverbal communication, which we will discuss below.

4. **Face to Face:** If it matters, say it in person. For issues of the heart and important messages, you need the advantage of body language cues.

It's easy for us to create false, elaborate narratives when we receive messages in written form. Was that message said with love, anger, or irritation? Is the person excited? Maybe, maybe not. Is the sender pleased with your work or disappointed? Depending strictly on word choice, that can be difficult to decipher. So, we fabricate a conclusion based not on what the message actually says, but what we think we know about that person or their tendencies.

No wonder we get hurt and hurt others so often through sending texts and email!

Decide on your intent and the importance of the conversation and determine the desired outcome, and then you can more effectively choose the best mode of communication. If it's not that important, send a text. If it's important, get face-to-face.

Take the time to answer the big question, "What do I want out of this?" before you send an important message via text or social media. Think carefully before you hit the send button. If you really want to make an impression, try a handwritten note sent by the old-fashioned U.S. mail. Whatever your choice, your written word is permanent, and you can never take it back. So, slow down and be intentional.

TELEGRAPH YOUR INTENT

The next part of effective communication is conveying your intentions to others. If you have to deliver some critique, for example, it is essential to let them know what to expect and why you are saying it.

The *fastest* way to shut down communication is to catch someone off guard.

I regularly preface corrective statements with, "This is coming from a place of love, not ego." Then I say what I need to say and check for understanding.

If you care enough about someone, you will be honest. Caring about your relationship means removing the filters and speaking the truth.

Human beings are complex, but we are also predictable. When someone delivers a message that we don't want to hear, whether that be a critique or a judgment, the walls go up and block effective communication. However, if you preface a statement with love and intent, it opens them up and prepares people for what you have to say.

This extra step is necessary if you want your words to be heard and correctly interpreted rather than deflected and misunderstood.

ASK, DON'T LABEL

Live long enough, and you come to expect certain kinds of people to act in specific, predictable ways. We base these predictions and assumptions on many things, from a person's age and physical appearance to their occupation and accessory choices.

We think we know people or can categorize them based on established criteria.

However, it turns out we are terrible at this.

Assumptions made based on first impressions are deceiving. Labels put strict limits on how much you can learn from other people, and they cloud the lens of communication so much that no one hears your real messages. In short, the whole process of labeling is problematic.

Have you ever been upset in public when around people who didn't know you? Do you think they assumed you are just an unhappy, bitter human being? Probably. But you know that's not the truth.

No one behaves or responds perfectly. It's impossible.

One way to avoid labeling is to dig a little before you stamp someone with an incorrect classification. For example, rather than assume a person is lazy because he or she didn't properly execute a task, ask them *why* they think things didn't go as planned. If they respond with, "I dunno. I think it's fine," then maybe laziness is to blame.

However, what if you give them a chance to be honest, and they say, "Well, I didn't fully understand my role, but I was too embarrassed to ask."

That's something you can work on together to improve! Next time, both parties will feel more confident and satisfied with the outcome.

A person's behavior does tend to define them. However, most people who get labeled as rude, lazy, or incompetent deserve for you to find out for yourself if this is really who they are, or if you are categorizing them by unfair and inaccurate labels.

If you are interested in shaking up the status quo and engaging in real, honest communication, check for understanding. Ask more questions!

If someone is rude, is it really directed at you? Probably not. People are hurting. If someone gives you subpar work, were the parameters clearly defined and expectations set? Likely not.

Most people are better, kinder, and smarter than we know. Sometimes we enter into conversations where we think we can accurately predict what someone is going to say. So, we give our programmed responses and allow preconceived assumptions to override what is really being said. Internally, we congratulate ourselves for being so intuitive and smart, but the truth is, we've been extremely irresponsible.

That kind of communication comes from a place of ego. Instead, choose to slow down and make it about listening better and helping them, not congratulating yourself on your (faulty) insight.

Maybe they're just having a bad day. Perhaps their intent is not what you've created in your mind. Ask questions, inquire deeper, and listen carefully. Don't presume or assume anything.

Curiosity can change the status quo. Ask the questions that no one else is asking. Don't be boring, and you won't get boring answers. When you do this, it's incredible how many of the original labels no longer fit.

THERE'S NO SUCH THING AS A LITTLE LIE

As I have mentioned before, I regularly tell my team, "You may not always like me, but you can always trust me." My communication is straightforward and game-free. It's not always what people want to hear, but they know it's the unfiltered truth.

Like most people, I do not fully lower my guard until I sense reciprocal trust and a mutual desire for what's best. You must earn trust. Once you do, however, you must still work to retain and deserve it.

Particularly in your home and workplace, if you don't have trust, you don't have honest communication. One of the most egregious trust destroyers is dishonesty. I'm not talking about the big lies. We all know those will destroy any relationship. I'm talking about little white lies.

Little lies can cause just as much trouble. Let's say I'm planning to extend my business trip by an extra day to go golfing. There's a chance my wife may not like the idea, so I decide not to tell her.

It's easier to ask for forgiveness than permission, right?

She may never find out, or she might. If she does, imagine the internal battle that will wage in her mind that might sound like, "If he's not telling me about a game of golf, what else is he not telling me about?"

It's not worth it. Ever.

Instead of hiding the truth about the length of the business trip, imagine if I approached my wife—my most trusted teammate in life—and said, "I'm thinking about playing golf with Brent during my trip next week. It would mean I'd be home Thursday afternoon instead of Wednesday evening. What do you think about that?"

The idea that it's easier to ask for forgiveness than permission *is* accurate. However, the saying shouldn't stop there. It should also include,

"It may be easier in the short run, but it makes your life so much harder in the long run."

You may be honest and not like the response you hear. That is still better than jeopardizing the most valuable thing in your relationships. Trust in any relationship is the key to winning.

Little lies are not little, and this applies across the board. There are not different sets of rules for home and work. The same rules about honesty apply when communicating with a hundred people or just one. It's imperative to be honest because otherwise, you're not being genuine.

I'll often hear someone say, "I wish I'd been able to say how I really feel."

Well then, why didn't you? What stopped you other than yourself?

We walk on eggshells, afraid of offending others, of stepping on toes, or perhaps even saying something with which (gasp!) someone else doesn't agree. We are not experts on how other people feel. We know what we believe, and we assume others think and feel the same.

I'll repeat it—we are really bad at guessing how others feel. Don't create stories in your head. Those are fantasy, never reality.

The most important thing is what you're doing in this moment. Not what happened in the past, not what may happen in the future, but right now. Instead of worrying about the what-ifs and creating imaginary scenarios, focus on being honest and genuine right now.

Sometimes you need to say things that are tough for others to hear and accept. However, you can feel satisfied knowing you delivered your message with authentic intentions.

WHAT YOU SAY WITHOUT WORDS

We've talked about words and how powerful they can be. As mighty as they are, nonverbal communication is even more powerful.

Communication was one of my college majors, and I remember there was never one decisive answer as to how much of a message we convey nonverbally. Some claim what we say without words accounts for 55 percent of a message, while others say it's as much as 70 or even 90 percent.

For better or for worse, we make snap judgments based on what we see. We are also far more likely to believe a person whose words match their body language. For example, if a friend met you for dinner to help you with a tough decision you have to make, but she continually checked her phone every time a notification popped up on the screen, would you feel like she was genuinely there to listen or had any real desire to help?

She may *say* she's listening, but you would doubt her intention based on what you *see*.

When I'm meeting with someone, I never want my words and my visual presence to conflict. In other words, I want my nonverbal communication to deliver my intent just as much as my verbal communication.

I make eye contact. I nod in agreement.

The most exceptional communicators are animated with their hands and use them to articulate their points because movement can create energy that is passed on to the audience. If I am on an urgent phone call, I don't stay seated. I get up and walk around to create extra energy.

If you've never tried it, you should. It can breathe new life into a critical conversation.

Our words may say the right things, but the body doesn't lie. People can sense when you're engaged, and they can also sense when you are not really listening and are just waiting for your turn to speak.

One way to stay fully committed to interactions is to ask more questions. If you ask questions during a conversation, it tells the other person you are tuned in. It also reminds you to pay attention and listen carefully so you can ask relevant questions.

In the classic book *How to Win Friends and Influence People*, Dale Carnegie puts it this way: "In order to be interesting, you have to be interested."

Be interested in what people have to say. If you ask questions and remain engaged, they will walk away with the distinct feeling that you are a wonderful human being. They may not be able to pinpoint why, but they will be sure of it. You know, and I know it's because you showed them genuine interest.

People want to be heard, so give that to them.

I will say it again: if it's crucial, have the conversation face to face. Phone calls are limiting. Without the benefit of seeing facial expressions and body language, you will not be able to fully interpret any message. All you have to judge the success of your communication is words. Remember, words can be manipulated, but body language doesn't lie.

BE CONCISE

If you open an email and it almost looks like someone typed out a book, do you groan a little? We all do.

Writing a long email is not completely our fault—we are conditioned to be wordy. From the time we learn to read and write, we learn to communicate in a set number of words.

It's not about effective communication.

It's about checking a box.

Did you write all 1,000 words of your 1,000-word essay? If you did, you get an A.

Did you write 600 words of your 1,000-word essay (even though you entirely made your point and executed it flawlessly)? If you didn't use 1,000 words, the best you can hope for is a C.

That's nuts—but what choice do we have? We want an A, so we do the dance and write the correct number of words.

When you say too much, you lose your audience, no matter how powerful or essential your message may be. When it comes to communication, less is often more. One of the most famous and impactful speeches in human history, the Gettysburg Address, is just 272 words long! It speaks to the power of being concise.

People appreciate it when you get to the point and don't waste their time. Why take 500 words to say something that could take 50 and be just as effective?

Being concise requires a little preparation because we ramble when we don't have a plan and have not set the intention. People may be conditioned to be wordy, but you can override your programming by taking the time to plan what you need to say.

Remove the fluff, stay on task without the tangents, and your message has a higher probability of getting through.

COMMUNICATION TROUBLESHOOTING

George Bernard Shaw once said, "The single biggest problem in communication is the illusion that it has taken place."

Many people go through life on autopilot. They say whatever comes into their mind, or they say what they've been programmed to speak, without thinking.

The saying "Life is not a dress rehearsal" is overused and hackneyed, but it is still correct and relevant to this discussion. Those conversations you are having with your kids, significant other, friends, co-workers —those aren't practice runs. Now is the time to hear and be heard. Not ten years from now. Today.

If you want to step back and assess how well you communicate, there are some simple ways to do that.

First, let's say you had a conversation with someone, and you left the meeting thinking you were crystal clear as to next steps. However, a few days later, the work you thought you had agreed to be done has not been completed.

What happened?

You could assume the person forgot or is just lazy. Alternatively, you could communicate effectively by asking what happened, in a direct but tactful way. So many people are scared to ask for help or clarification on assignments because they don't want to be labeled as incompetent or unintelligent.

If you want X out of a conversation, and it always turns into Y, the problem is not everyone else. You and your communication style are the only common denominators. Do the work of an authentic leader and check for understanding. If miscommunication occurred, the only way to productively fix it is to first address it, not sweep it under the rug or point fingers.

Do you know anyone who seems to be a drama magnet? What about that friend who complains about the constant fights with their significant other? People like this frequently follow their complaints with comments like, "Why does drama always seem to find me?"

If you experience the same communication breakdowns over and over, once again, it's time to consider that maybe *other people* aren't the issue. It's time to look in the mirror. Resolve to communicate your intent and become more aware of your body language when you speak. If you are expecting a fight, your body will tense up, your face will sour, and everything about your nonverbals will say, "Let's get ready to rumble."

If you'd like to lessen the amount of conflict you encounter, become aware of your triggers (what sets you off) and how you can control your responses to them. Stating your intent out of the gate is always the best. With time and intention, you can *do* better and *be* better for those around you.

We may not be able to control how others interpret our messages, but we can do everything at our end of the communication to remove as much of the guesswork, assumptions, and conjecture as possible.

Stating what you want out of a conversation and creating a place of trust where you and others can be open are the keys to successful communication. If you establish a safe place for trust to occur, it will save time and frustration, and it will strengthen relationships rather than make them weaker.

You bring biases, moods, and more into each interaction. Those only serve to obscure your messages, hurt feelings, and cause widespread miscommunication.

Not everybody's going to agree with you. That's not the point of communication. The point is to transmit your message successfully and to give others the space to do the same.

LET'S GO WIN

"Selflessness is humility.
Humility and freedom
go hand in hand.
Only a humble person
can be free."
JEFF WILSON

· *Nine* ·

HUMILITY

T he word *ego* has an almost universally negative connotation. We associate it with entitlement and arrogance.

And yet, we all have one.

Egos serve a distinct purpose. If we didn't have an ego, we would become mentally unstable. That's because our ego helps mediate between the unconscious and the conscious.

It also tends to magnify both our best and worst traits. That's one of the reasons ego got its bad rap; it tricks us into believing that the most amplified version of ourselves is our sole identity.

For example, let's say you have studied extensively how to be a leader. You read all the books, got the right degrees at the best schools, and steadily rose in the ranks of your company, receiving plenty of recognition along the way. Now, you are a widely respected, top-level executive.

Your ego puts that into a box and slaps a label on it that says, "World

Class Leader." When you've listened to that self-led narrative for long enough, you start to believe you are pretty darn remarkable.

Are you known for your hilarious jokes? Your ego decides you are officially the funniest friend in your circle. Your kids turn out well? You are the best and wisest parent of all your friends. Publish a few successful books? You are a creative and talented writer.

Fill in the blank—whenever you shine, your ego starts to run the show by default. After a while, you identify yourself solely through your ego, and preserving that gilded image becomes an all-consuming obsession.

The irony is that while believing you are the best and the brightest may seem like a confidence booster, it does more harm than good because it creates the unquenchable need to compare yourself to others. That's when you start to keep up with the Joneses; you judge, and you compete.

When your ego perceives that someone is smarter, stronger, better, or happier, you become increasingly bitter and frustrated. Your ego has deceived you into believing that you *are* that label—and when you start to lose that label, you lose yourself. Colin Powell, the retired general and former Secretary of State, said it this way: "Never let your ego get so close to your position that when your position goes, your ego goes with it."

At the other end of the spectrum, *humility* is when we are profoundly aware of our strengths and our weaknesses. It's knowing full well what our talents and our weaknesses are, and then intentionally removing the need to make it all about "me, me, me."

Humility is acknowledging our ego and then checking it at the door.

Humility is not believing our own hype.

There is no denying we live in a self-absorbed society. We are each tuned into WII-FM (the "What's In It For Me?" channel) 24 hours a day. We also think that to make something of ourselves, we have to believe we are the best, to visualize personal success, and to live according to all the other achievement mantras we hear.

I'm not knocking confidence. However, there is an enormous difference between *confidence* and *egotism*.

I am a confident person. In my days of playing sports, I was borderline cocky. Thankfully, I also learned at a young age that the best athletes are team players rather than solo performers.

The power of teamwork is evident across the board—from sports, to business, to personal relationships. If you want the team (sports team, work team, family) to be successful, the focus has to be on everyone.

How do you fight the tendency to make it all about you? The answer, once again, rests with intention. Become awake to and aware of those natural inclinations to think highly of yourself and less of others. Eckhart Tolle says that "the moment you become aware of the ego in you, it is strictly no longer the ego but just an old, conditioned mind pattern. Ego implies unawareness. Awareness and ego cannot co-exist."

What do you want out of a relationship, meeting, game, or interaction? If you approach this question from a place of ego, you become a person who is known to put *you* and *your* needs first—and let's be honest:

No one wants to be around that person.

Think about the classic movie *Titanic*. There are two types of people who reveal their most authentic selves when that ship starts to sink: There are the ego-driven people who scramble for the lifeboats, knocking over women and children along the way. Then, there are people who put their own needs aside in order to help others.

Thankfully, in the real lives most of us lead, shelving our ego doesn't mean we have to go down with the ship. In fact, it usually means that we experience more satisfaction and less drama. We can remove ourselves from the rat race and instead love others.

If you want the best for those around you, those people will stand in line to be in your sphere. You will never be without friends. You'll have vastly fulfilling relationships.

The practice of humility is quite simply a better way to go through life.

ME VS. WE

Big egos destroy relationships and ruin companies. Husbands and wives want to satisfy their own requirements, and they forget there is another human being in the relationship with valid wants and needs. Friends need help, and they neglect their friends who may be hurting, too. Ambitious CEOs get a taste of success and forget about all the people who made that success possible.

People become so focused on their personal headlines that they invent a narrative and conclude they have done more than their business partner or spouse to make a business or their marriage work.

Maybe you *did* contribute more, but who really cares who is responsible? Isn't it more fun to share the spotlight? Harry S. Truman said, "It's amazing what can be accomplished if no one cares who gets the credit."

Hogging the credit is unproductive and short-sighted. On the other hand, when you approach tasks, work, and life with an attitude of collaboration, you will accomplish so much more.

Let's say a successful idea was almost entirely yours. Great! Share that victory with others, because, why not? Show others what humility looks like by not requiring everyone to know just how much of a role you played. Chances are, the right people know anyway and if they don't, you can still feel satisfied knowing that you contributed to the success of others.

Steve Jobs was a visionary who unquestionably accomplished world-changing things. He was also known to walk all over other people. Perhaps his vision was so big that he didn't think he could afford the luxury of considering how others felt. He had plans to change the world, and so he did what was necessary.

The thing is, people will seldom remember what you said, but they'll always remember how you made them feel. Jobs did change the world, but he undoubtedly charred a lot of his personal and professional relationships in the process.

Another example of this is Terrell Owens. There is no doubt he is one of the best football players who ever played the game. However, he was not a favorite among his teammates. He was more like a Steve Jobs or a Steve Ballmer (spotlight takers) than a Warren Buffett or a Bill Gates (team players).

Tom Brady, on the other hand, approaches the game in a way that has never been rivaled. He is loved and highly admired by his teammates. He's also considered by most to be the greatest football player of all time.

Brady checks his ego and practices humility when most other people in his position might choose to bask in the glory. Ultimately, people see him and his talent on full display, and no one has any doubt of his tremendous skill. They also know that *he* knows he'd be nothing without his teammates and his coaches.

To me, the outcome of both of these men's careers says it all. Terrell Owens has never won a championship. He didn't even go to his own Hall of Fame ceremony. Tom Brady, on the other hand, has already won more Super Bowl championships than any other quarterback in history.

My best sport was swimming, but it was my least favorite of all my athletic interests. My wins were all up to me. Sure, we had a team and we had relays, but in the water, it was every man for himself. For someone who thrives on the energy of a team environment, that was torture.

In a healthy relationship, there is never one person who is responsible for all the good or all the bad. It always takes two (or more) to tango. At work, there are no great successes that rest solely on the shoulders of one single person.

This book is an example of how the power of the collective surpasses the power of one. My name is on the cover, but that's not the whole story. So many people indirectly helped write this book—my wife, children, parents, grandparents, siblings, authors whose books I've read, mentors, co-workers, business partners, and friends. They've all shaped my experiences and therefore, have contributed significantly to the lessons I've learned.

If you were to ask people on their deathbeds if they were solely responsible for their most significant successes in life, it'd be difficult to find anyone who would say yes. And if they *did* think their wins were all up to them, I can guarantee you they lived an overwhelmingly lonely existence.

Have you ever heard of a kid who hopes that no one will come to his birthday party? Of course not! Who wants to celebrate alone? Imagine celebrating all by yourself, and then imagine celebrating with dozens of people. Can you feel the energy difference between those two? It's more fun to be surrounded by friends!

Start practicing humility today by replacing *me* and *I* with *we* and *us*. Communicate to your teammates that you value them and show them that you see their contributions by speaking about the collective team. Replace your ego with actions and reactions that come from a place of love.

INTERESTING VS. INTERESTED

You may remember this quote from the last chapter, but it deserves to be repeated. As Dale Carnegie said, "In order to be interesting, you have to be interested."

If you have ever gotten into a conversation with an egocentric person, you know this feeling all too well: a pit in your stomach starts to build as they talk and talk and talk. They drone on about their victories and achievements, in their minds thinking that they must sound like "The Most Interesting Man in the World."

Yeah, not so much.

Pretend you are interested in asking someone out on a date. You walk up and introduce yourself. For the next 15 minutes, you unload on this unwitting individual how successful and amazing you are. Then, you stop to take a breath and ask, "So, would you like to go out sometime?"

Would you be surprised if this person turned you down? You shouldn't be. No one wants to go out with a real-life, ego-driven Chatty Kathy or Chatty Karl doll.

No one wants to be within a hundred feet of a person who is singing their own praises.

Instead, what if you walked up to this person and asked them about their life and interests, and then you listened? Your request for a date would be far better received.

Overtalking is a common mistake in the business world, particularly in sales. Salespeople will jump right into their spiel and neglect to determine whether prospects even need the product or service they are selling.

Don't product dump.

Ask and be interested in what your prospects have to say.

Humility is what fosters excellent relationships because when you don't make it about yourself, you slow down long enough to stop talking. That's when other people understand that you care about them—and that will make them trust you, like you, and respect you.

Humility is letting go of the desire to have others know how special you are. The ironic part is they *will* think you are the most special person on the planet if you allow them the opportunity to speak and to also form their own opinion.

It's so easy to talk about ourselves because this is the only reality we know. It's all we have. Many of us also have an innate drive to let other people know what we have accomplished—and there is nothing wrong with that.

The thing is, everyone else feels the same way.

When you enter into a conversation, don't think, "What's in it for me?" Instead think, "What can I do for others?" When you practice humility, you may not be the star of the conversation. Instead, you'll become the guide—and that's a fun and rewarding role to play.

WHAT VS. WHY

It's easy for us to judge what is in front of us, to take what we see at face value and draw conclusions. If you want to practice humility, you must avoid making it about *what* is going on instead of focusing on the *why*.

More companies are starting to understand the importance of this and are acting with a bigger and more powerful *why* as the driving force. When there's a more significant cause that everyone is working toward, it makes all the hard work that much more rewarding.

One company that operates with *why-focused* goals is TOMS. For every pair of shoes sold, they give a pair of shoes to someone in need in underdeveloped countries. Warby Parker does the same thing, but with eyeglasses. For every headband and flower crown sold, Headbands of Hope provides a headband to a child battling pediatric cancer.

There is so much good in the world, and that good is always centered on a powerful why. When your focus is on the *why* (a purpose bigger than yourself), then the *what* (the tangible reward you get) seems so much less essential.

One of the most extreme examples of the adverse effects of *what-focused* vision is the rise and fall of Lee Iacocca. Undoubtedly one of the greatest names in car manufacturing, Iacocca was also famously all about himself. At age 46, he became the president of Ford Motor Company in 1970. Despite plenty of success, he was fired less than a decade later by Henry Ford II, who despised Iacocca's ego.

He was later named chairman at Chrysler, where he continued his expert but egotistical ways. He was so terrified of being bested by anyone that he fired some of his most talented team members so they would never be able to steal any of the glory or, worse still, his job.

Japanese carmakers began transforming the industry, but Iacocca failed to stay ahead of the changes. He thought he knew it all. So, instead of adopting state-of-the-art processes and modernizing manufacturing, he began alienating his designers and engineers by making arbitrary changes to vehicles based on whims and irrational ego-driven motives.

There is no doubt that Iacocca was a great businessman, but his self-centered focus and egocentric ways cost him dearly. By 1992, he was forced out of Chrysler. Despite a few attempts to get back in (including a botched takeover), his efforts fell flat, and he retired with a tarnished reputation.

You may have some success in the short term when you operate according to what you, personally, stand to gain—when you are driven by ego and focus only on what rewards you can achieve for yourself. Eventually, however, the people who helped to make you successful will grow tired of working with someone who has misaligned values.

The *why* matters.

In fact, according to the most recent surveys, the majority of employees rank meaningfulness as the number-one contributor to on-the-job happiness, outranking recognition, opportunity, and even salary.

Help others see the bigger picture by showing them that you care about more than your own needs—practice humility to allow the *why* to inspire more decisions.

FAULT VS. FEELINGS

Our ego is one of the primary drivers of our tendency to label. We label ourselves; we label others. In the pursuit of glory, recognition, being right, justifying our actions, or defending our choices, we judge and place people into definable, limiting categories.

We also love to assign blame. Did a new idea fail at work? It's your co-worker's fault. Is the fuel on empty when you are running late? It's your spouse's fault. Did you stub your toe on a misplaced chair? It's the kids' fault.

That's your ego thinking for you.

Check these types of responses, and instead transform your reactions into something productive. For example, if my wife loses her temper, I could judge her reaction and label her a hothead. But what does this do other than hamper further communication and shut us both down?

Instead, what if I stopped and said, "When we yell, both of us get defensive. Can we talk rather than shout because we're friends, not enemies?"

If you throw out a label (you're such a jerk, idiot, or worse), their ego will respond right back with a label for you. Now you've made the problem worse. When it comes to your loved ones, you can learn how to put your defenses down (and help them do the same) by removing your ego's needs to be right and (wrongly) place blame.

In the end, nothing gets accomplished when you point fingers. Take a step or two back and consider what you want to achieve in an interaction. When it comes to relationships in your life that really matter, there can be no ego battles if you're going to be the person your family, friends, and co-workers need.

APATHY VS. ACTION

Throughout this chapter, I've referred to the "practice" of humility, because it's an act. It's something that you can become better at the more you practice it. There are three steps you can take to be humble in a real and practical way: learn, apply, and reflect.

Learn. First, you can never stop learning, and a big part of that is conscious observation. Are you quick to label and place blame? Why does your ego default to that? Start to become more aware of how your ego dictates your thoughts and reactions. Learn about yourself— it sounds simple, but it's a lifelong process.

Start to learn what actions produce desired results. For example, if you ask your children to clean their room and they ask why, what happens when you give the typical, ego-driven, "Because I said so!" parent response? The work may get done, but you'll have to try just as hard and gripe just as much the next time.

But what happens when you give the real reason? When your kids ask why, try something like, "Because you must grow up to be the kind of people who clean up after themselves. Messy roommates, co-workers, and spouses cause all kinds of unnecessary issues, and I want you to take responsibility for the footprints you make in life."

The goal my wife and I have set as parents is to raise good people who contribute to the world, and my ego's reasoning ("because I said so") is counterproductive. Help your kids trust you by being humble and leading with the *why*.

Apply. Now comes the hard part. Practicing humility is one of those things that sounds great but can be challenging in the heat of the moment. When tempers flare, or your ego perceives some injustice or an opportunity to shine, it may try to take over. Remember that the best interactions are those in which you give more than you get. Give—over and over again.

Reflect. When you interact with someone, assess the results. Intentionally approach life ready to learn from both the successes and the missteps. Reflect on how much of a role your ego has played and how that has affected the outcome.

Be quiet and listen to the different narratives playing out in your head. Do that a sufficient number of times, and you can more easily decipher which narratives are ego-driven and which are coming from a place of humility.

You have a choice—you can be the kind of person who makes a beeline for the next open spot on the lifeboat, or you can stop and help others put on their life jackets correctly. Those are two extremes, but they represent what it looks like when your ego is driving the ship versus humility.

Ego is self. Humility is others.

Be an "others" kind of person. You will enjoy life so much more.

LET'S GO WIN

"If it's not fun,
you're not doing it right."
BOB BASSO

· *Ten* ·

FUN

Everywhere you look, there's nothing but a sea of unhappy, somber faces.

Glance around your office. Peek into a store as you walk by its windows. Take a look inside the vehicle next to you at the traffic light. You'll find an assortment of grumpy, serious expressions that range from boredom all the way to rage.

To observe the polar opposite collection of emotions and faces, walk into a kindergarten classroom. Two kids are quietly humming to themselves. Another girl is dancing and twirling without any music playing. A group of kids is laughing hysterically for some unspecified reason.

Granted, a typical American five-year-old's list of woes and worries is pretty short. There's impending bedtime, the annoying task of teeth brushing, only getting one cookie instead of two—and that's about it.

On the other hand, if you ask the typical American adult to list their woes and worries, you better pull up a chair, because you're going to be there for a while.

You take on more responsibility as you age. This is a natural progression if you intend to become a responsible grown-up who contributes to society.

Unfortunately, somewhere along the way, life gets so serious that fun becomes a foreign feeling. A steady and unrelenting mix of insecurities, responsibilities, and judgment programs us to replace joy with drudgery.

Sorry, but I'm not buying it. I refuse to accept that fun must stop once we reach adulthood. Fun does not have an expiration date.

If it's not fun, I'm not doing it.

How could a grown man with a family and responsibilities say such a thing? Because fun is a choice. No matter the task, no matter the amount of work required, you can intentionally choose to find the pleasure in life's tasks. The way I see it is this:

If you have to do it anyway, it might as well be enjoyable.

MAKE FUN THE STANDARD

Being a kid is a pretty sweet gig. Children can say, "I'm hungry," and a few minutes later, they have food. Kids get to drink juice from a box. They are allowed to be silly with no judgment. They can make funny faces and happily skip from point A to point B without being branded as strange.

Then we grow up, and it's as though some mysterious power banishes all fun from our daily work and life routine. Smiles and laughter become scarce commodities.

When you see an adult belly-laughing in a restaurant or on the subway, it's like witnessing a white tiger in the wild—a rarity that fills you with astonishment and curiosity. Wide-eyed onlookers wonder to themselves:

"What could that man possibly find so funny that he's willing to make a fool of himself by laughing, unreservedly, in public?"

As you get older, you become increasingly aware of all the eyes watching and judging you. For most, it starts in high school. Your peers decide what's fashionable and accepted—and being goofy and silly usually doesn't make the cut.

I fell victim to peer pressure as most people do, but in my early twenties, I had an epiphany:

Who the heck cares?

Why am I so concerned about what others think? My real friends already accept me and love me just as I am, so why lose a moment's sleep over what anyone else thinks?

From then on, I determined never to waste a single day of my life by approaching work as an endless and challenging inventory of tasks to be completed.

There have been times in my career when I have buckled down and buried my nose in work. Those periods were the darkest times of my life, times when I felt isolated and disconnected from family and friends.

I realize now that it's just not worth it.

I still work hard, but these days I have a lot more fun while I'm at it, and I fully expect everyone who works alongside me to have fun as well. I want to hear laughter all day. I want to see smiles.

Having fun is one of our core company values. I've never had one single person tell me they'd like to experience *less* enjoyment at work.

I live according to the same guidelines at home. I could totally dread housework—or I could have fun! Take vacuuming, for example. Whether I choose to enjoy it or not, I still have to vacuum. I can't close my eyes and magically compel the stand-up vacuum to run on its own, or make the dishes load themselves into the dishwasher while I put my feet up and binge-watch on Netflix.

I could decide that the next 30 minutes of vacuuming will be sheer torture, or I could put on my headphones and have a vacuum dance party.

I'll choose a dance party every time.

Fun is the standard in my life, not the exception. It's infused into my routine as much as the air I breathe.

GAMIFY YOUR WORKDAY

Famed author Roald Dahl once wrote, "Life is more fun if you play games."

I couldn't agree more. If you think your workday is a grind, it will be a grind. If you dread the busywork, the meetings, the water-cooler gossip, and the memos, you will live a life of *less*.

Less fun, less laughter, less everything.

However, there is a way to live a life of *more*, and it's called gamification.

We are wired to compete and have fun. How many hours can the typical teenage boy spend playing video games? What about casinos?

You lose track of all time and reason when you are inside one.

Gamification is when you apply the elements of traditional game playing (such as point scoring, competition, and rules of gameplay) to other areas of activity that are not generally associated with fun.

Early in my career, I used to make a tremendous amount of outbound sales calls to set appointments. That is not what most people would call fun. My friend and co-worker Nathan and I decided to gamify the activity. We'd determine prizes for who set the most appointments that day, and whoever won got the big payoff. For example, the losing guy would have to wash the other one's car (none of the incentives involved money because we were both young and broke).

Once we had made it a game rather than a task, we got excited about it! Can you imagine being enthusiastic about making a sales call? I can tell you it's possible because I lived it.

The best part is the game element made cold calling even more productive. I approached each new conversation with a greater purpose, and that intention came through on my calls. I spoke with a smile on my face, and my prospects could hear that. They benefited, and so did I.

Dale Carnegie said, "People rarely succeed unless they have fun in what they are doing." Fun increases your odds of winning! So, decide to have a good time. You have to do the work anyway, so you can either drudge through it and be miserable, or you can do the same task with a smile on your face—and end the day feeling great.

It's that simple.

CHOOSE YOUR PERSPECTIVE

I heard a story about a prominent businessman named Steve Collins who had a heart attack, and while he was in open-heart surgery to have a bypass, he had a stroke. Because of the stroke, he was left permanently paralyzed and in a wheelchair. Steve loves to start out his conversations with:

> *"The bad news is I had a heart attack, and then I had a stroke, and now I'm paralyzed. But the good news is, I had a heart attack, and then I had a stroke, and now I'm paralyzed."*

He could have died after the heart attack or after the stroke. He could have lost the ability to speak on top of the paralysis. Or the motivation and drive to function at all. But he didn't. He is alive, and he is so grateful.

That's an inspiring perspective.

As Hans Christian Andersen said, "Enjoy life. There's plenty of time to be dead." Life may be hard right now—but you are alive. You are here, and you can still make choices while you have breath in your body.

Lisa and I recently attended a memorial service. The family tried their best to make it a celebration of life by telling stories about their loved one who had passed, but there was nothing but sadness everywhere we looked.

At the reception, we turned to each other and almost simultaneously said, "When one of us dies, let's throw a party. There needs to be laughter and smiles as we remember all the good times and fun. Let's truly celebrate life."

That's not to say mourning and tears are not okay. Because they are *more* than okay; they are a necessary part of the grieving process. Even in death, however, I want to be responsible for making people smile because that is how I'm living my life.

Perspective is the key. I hear busy professionals and parents complain about their fast-paced, hectic schedules. Moms and dads with multiple kids playing multiple sports often say they feel like a taxi service—and I get it.

Time is both valuable and fleeting, and it's hard to feel like you are getting the most out of life at the pace you are moving. However, if you have chosen to stack your schedule, and if quitting or cutting back on activities is off the table, you have only two options:

1. Complain about your choices and stew in your grumblings.
2. Accept your choices and enjoy the ride.

It's all about perspective, which means it comes down to which option you embrace. In other words, you can say, "The *bad* news is I've been driving my kids around all day," or you can choose to say, "The *good* news is I've been driving my kids around all day."

That one little word change makes a world of difference.

FILL YOUR BUCKETS

As we age, we become crippled by the increasing awareness of what it takes to maintain the right image. The next time you go to a wedding, notice the 4- and 5-year-old children dancing with pure abandon at the reception, while the middle-aged men and women either sit it out or do the "barely dance" (where you are standing on the dance floor but barely moving).

We become ashamed to do something that feels so natural—to move our bodies to the music.

If you can relate to that, you are not alone. But if the idea of shaking it on the dance floor is too much to bear, at least start dancing at home. For those of you who legitimately don't like dancing, then find something, *anything,* that makes you feel like a kid again.

Forget what anybody else thinks or feels. It's about enjoyment.

Here's the thing about all work and no play—it leaves too many of your buckets empty. Recall the areas of life that we discussed earlier in the book: spirituality, health, significant other, family, friends, mission, finances, energy, emotion, and adventure. Whenever you are deficient in any one of these, all the other pieces suffer.

Fun is the foundation that keeps all of these areas healthy. When it's missing, nothing works as well as it should. Let's say you're a responsible parent, provider, and spouse. You check all the boxes on paper, and you do and say all the right things. But you still feel hollow.

You're missing the fun! There's fun at work (gamification), fun with your family (family game night, vacations), fun with your significant other (date night), solo fun (a hobby), and fun with friends (guys' or girls' night). When one or more of these is lacking, that will bleed into all other areas of your life.

Also, find a little adventure. It's a vital part of being a complete human being. No matter how hectic life has become for you, you deserve to have your buckets filled to the brim with enjoyment and excitement.

BE LIKE THE NAKED OLD GUY

Most of us are looking for our place in the world. We want to fit in, and we don't want to ruffle feathers or get labeled. We also want other people to know how hard we work and how many sacrifices we make.

I've been there.

But, these days, I'm more like the naked old guy in the gym locker room.

If you have ever been to a group locker room, you may have seen the phenomenon of the naked old guy. He's that older man who walks around naked as a jaybird as he dries his hair, shaves, carries on full conversations, and lounges in the sauna. He's out there for the world to see and doesn't seem to be in any hurry to put on pants.

He's lived long enough to realize that if he wants to air dry his birth-day suit, who's going to stop him? Onlookers may quietly wish he'd grab a towel or throw on some boxers. But that guy? He is who he is, and he's not going to change.

You have to admire the naked old guy. I prefer to cover up in the locker room, but in life, I no longer hide who I am. I love to enjoy my days, and I do not care what judgmental strangers think about that decision.

Television commercials and movies showcase the big things in life—graduating from school, falling in love, getting married, having kids, landing your dream career, going on lavish vacations. For sure, those momentous occasions are noteworthy.

But let's be real—97 percent of life is made up of the small things, like going to bed, waking up, making dinner, watching TV, mowing the lawn, and driving to work.

If you think about it, the small things *are* the big things.

If we trudge through the small things just waiting for the next significant experience, life is going to be much less joyful than it should be. You can choose right now to enjoy life, from the mundane to the majestic. Remember, it's all about perspective!

For example, packing your suitcase for a vacation doesn't have to be a chore. If you've got a family, you are packing a bag to make memories with them—memories your kids will be telling their kids one day.

That is a real privilege and a luxury.

We robotically go through life, and suddenly, we wake up ten years down the road. To us, it felt like ten minutes has just passed.

The days are long, but the years are short. Remember that the next time you find yourself dreading the grind or rolling your eyes when the kids ask you for water at bedtime for the millionth time. Enjoy the small things in life, because they are your life.

When we are young, we have fun with reckless abandon. When we are old, we stop caring about what other people think and let it all hang out. The problem is all those years in between when we are so darn serious, self-conscious, and judgmental.

It's time to let those pointless feelings go. It's time to be a little bit more like the 4-year-old on the dance floor or the naked old guy in the locker room (metaphorically speaking).

We allow stress and worry to rob us. We stress about being late, but we end up being right on time. Our socks don't match, but no one even noticed. The big project at work is behind schedule, but the boss extends the deadline three days before it was due.

Life has a way of working itself out.

So, what did all the worry do? Nothing except rob us of precious minutes, days, weeks, months, or even years of our life. Moments we will never be able to get back.

There is no reason to live in regret over the time you may have spent worrying or dreading tasks. You can decide today, right now, to have more fun.

Get a hobby, make plans to have dinner with a good friend, volunteer at your favorite nonprofit. Make time to pursue a hobby that may or may not make the world a better place. Just do it because you can and because you enjoy it.

In the immortal words of Dr. Seuss, "If you never did, you should. These things are fun, and fun is good."

"Courage is the
most important of
all virtues, because
without courage,
you can't practice
any other virtue
consistently."
MAYA ANGELOU

· *Eleven* ·

COURAGE

Fear is powerful. It prevents us from being *vulnerable*. It stifles a healthy *culture*. It causes us to overcomplicate things and behave in ways that are the antithesis of *simplicity*. It blocks us from starting beneficial *routines* because we are too scared to take action.

It takes *intention* and *accountability* and throws them out the window. It inhibits us from enjoying the present moment or practicing *mindfulness*. It shuts down effective *communication*. It transforms *humility* into false bravado. It completely destroys any chance to find the *fun*.

In other words, the different qualities we have discussed cannot manifest in the presence of fear. Fear holds you hostage. What you need instead is courage.

Because courage conquers fear every time.

Courage is a muscle that gets stronger the more you use it, but you have to be willing to put yourself out there once.

And then again.

And then again.

Courage enables you to stand for the values that mean the most to you. Courage allows others to hold you accountable for your words and actions. Courage will enable you to be vulnerable and authentic and to engage in effective communication. Then, once you are living and communicating without pretense and false bravado, a whole new world of possibility is revealed. It's a life full of fun and love.

Who doesn't want more of that?

You may have a good idea of what it takes to live the life you imagine, but it all comes down to how willing you are to be bold. Are you ready to face what is holding you back? Let's find out.

FEAR'S ROLE IN BEING COURAGEOUS

When you are standing on one side, looking over a vast chasm, the journey to the other side can seem dangerous, maybe even impossible. The part of you that resists change and wants to stay safe and comfortable whispers, "This is too risky. Let's turn back."

The problem is, everything you want is on the other side of that chasm.

Fear is what keeps you from taking that leap, so you must eliminate the fear to move forward, right?

If only it were that simple.

It'd be naïve to say you don't feel fear or that it's feasible to live the rest of your life without that familiar feeling rising up in you. Fear is normal, and it's okay to be afraid. The key is how you react to it.

People tend to feel ashamed of their fears. However, the reality is that without doubt and fear, there is no courage.

In other words, when you feel brave, it's because you also feel fear.

While fear plays a critical role in your life, it differs significantly from bravery. *Courage* is a conscious decision to act in spite of fear. On the other hand, fear itself is not a decision or act usually based on reality or truth. As its famous acronym reminds us, fear stands for:

False

Evidence

Appearing

Real.

However, fear is very real in terms of its influence on development, progress, and overall contentment. It limits people and keeps them from pursuing their dreams.

Everyone gets touched by fear. The question is, what are you going to do about it? Those who win are the ones who can acknowledge their fear and move ahead anyway.

The first time you tell fear to take a back seat, you may not feel confident about that decision. The second time you flex your courage muscles, however, you'll feel better about the choice. Do it again, and you start to feel noticeably braver.

Behaving with courage becomes more natural and comfortable with time and intention.

To clarify, I'm not talking about overcoming your fear of spiders or heights (although those are both valid fears). I'm talking about having the courage to speak up at work when you disagree with a new policy.

Having the courage to tell your spouse the truth about something that is bothering you.

Having the courage to get back into the gym even though you are embarrassed about how out of shape you have become.

Having the courage to tell your kids that you fully support them pursuing their dreams despite secretly fearing they'll end up disappointed.

Having the courage to admit you are not living your best life.

Address those fears out loud, just once, and they start to lose a little of their power. Do it over and over again, and they no longer have a foothold in your life.

That is when you are free!

Yes, there will always be new fears to replace old ones, but as long as you keep flexing your courage muscles and make it a daily practice, you can take on anything. You can start doing that today. Make the decision, "I'm going to go face this," and then act!

COURAGEOUS VS. FOOLHARDY

Courage can be one of your most valuable allies. If you flex your courage muscles correctly, you will be unstoppable. But there's a fine line between being courageous and being foolhardy. The word "foolhardy" is a combination of *fool* and *hardy*, which is a synonym for brave or bold. So, it's a form of bravery, but it's reckless or foolish bravery.

It's not admirable or respectable to be reckless.

It's just plain stupid.

Unfortunately, recklessness is relatively common, thanks in part to the commonly accepted idea that asking for help is a sign of weakness. We get this notion in our heads that we have to go it alone to prove ourselves.

Who determined this ridiculous standard?

A great example of this is the stereotype that men refuse to ask for directions. I confess I have been guilty of refusing to stop and ask for help before the days of GPS. What I didn't realize is that saying, "I don't know where I'm going. Can you help me?" is a display of courage, not weakness.

It doesn't take courage to drive aimlessly around in circles.

It's more courageous to ask for help, but it's also tough for us to skirt that fine line between appearing capable and admitting when we need help. This is because asking for help makes us feel vulnerable.

Great leaders are masters at this. In fact, it's the primary reason they become great leaders in the first place. Foolhardy leaders who pretend they can do it all end up crashing and burning. The bigger problem is when they do crash, they may sink the whole ship. Reckless leaders in the corporate world have been known to destroy companies and everything else within their orbit.

It is both egotistical and naïve to believe you can do it all. Have the courage to feel confident enough in yourself and your abilities to say, "I need other people to help me succeed, and I am more than willing to share the credit."

Think about these two contrasting images. First, imagine you are contemplating a 30-foot jump into the water. Assuming the water is sufficiently deep, you know how to swim, and there are no rocks in the way, you can do this safely, aided by a little courage.

Now, imagine contemplating a 30-foot jump onto concrete. That takes courage, too.

But it's also idiotic.

There is an inherent lack of intention associated with reckless behavior. Ask yourself, "Is this the right thing to do, or am I letting my ego call the shots?"

The point is to be courageous but also intentional. That will help you avoid reckless or foolhardy behavior.

COURAGE AT WORK

Being courageous at work can be the hardest thing in the world to do. This is particularly true if you work in an office that doesn't openly encourage honesty and transparency.

Let's say you decide it's time to be heard. You tell your boss something he doesn't want to hear, but it's also something that will significantly benefit the company.

He doesn't take your honesty well. He threatens you, demotes you, or fires you. Or possibly worse, he starts to mistreat you and encourages others to do the same.

Maybe you should have just kept your mouth shut. Did your courage backfire?

Not at all. This insight is a blessing. If you cannot speak your mind, it may be time to move on to greener pastures. Sometimes, we have to make those hard decisions—and that can take a tremendous amount of courage.

It takes courage to speak your truth, and it takes humility to hear the truth. In the past, my business partner has said things to me that were hard to hear. It's never easy to take criticism, but I'm always better for it! I applaud him for his honesty. Being straightforward takes courage.

If you want to encourage others to be open and brave, be open to accepting what they have to say and thank them for it! Yes, *thank* someone for their criticism. It sounds hard, and it certainly can be. But it's also highly impactful.

Have the courage and put yourself out there. Courage is an attractive trait to the right employers, and if you get penalized for honesty at your current job, it's probably not the right job.

If you don't love your work, perhaps it's time to find something you do love. If you do love your job, cut your superiors a little slack and give them some time to react correctly. They are not in your shoes and probably don't know the ins and outs of what you do all day long. If they respect you and you respect them, professionally suggest changes, and hopefully, they will hear you and respond appropriately.

A great example of how this works is the television show *Undercover Boss*. If you've never seen it, you should because it's absolutely fascinating. Heads of companies will go undercover in their own businesses to see what their employees really think about company policies and procedures.

Invariably, in every episode, the boss discovers some kink in the system that needs to be repaired. After the big reveal, the boss asks the employee why that person never came forward and told anyone about the issue. The employee will say, "Well, I did, and it wasn't well received," or "I didn't feel like I could be honest with my manager."

You don't have to wait for the head of your company to go undercover. If you believe in yourself, have the courage to say it not once, not twice, but as many times as it takes.

Success rarely happens on the first try—but it takes courage to keep going.

Milton Hershey failed over and over again before he founded his wildly successful chocolate company. At first, he thought he wanted to be a printer and went to work for a newspaper. He hated it.

Next, he landed a job at a candy factory. After a few years there, he decided to open his own candy business, but he was forced to close a short time later due to lack of profits.

After that, he learned how to make caramels and opened up a business selling caramel candies on the streets of New York City. That also failed.

He returned to the farming hills of his childhood and decided to take a different approach. He looked around at the easily accessible and abundant supply of fresh dairy milk, and he started making milk chocolate. Within ten years, Milton Hershey built a gigantic chocolate factory and a whole town to go with it, Hershey, Pennsylvania.

When Macy's founder, R.H. Macy, was 15, he left home to work on a whaling ship. After four long years at sea, he returned to his hometown to work in his father's shop. He didn't want to live in his dad's shadow, so he opened his own needle-and-thread store. It quickly failed, and so did the dry goods store he tried next.

He spent some time working in his brother-in-law's shop before running off to pan for gold in California during the 1849 gold rush. After failing to find any gold, he returned home and opened up another store along with his brother. That one failed too!

Imagine the courage it must have taken to try once again to open up another store. But Macy did! He relocated to New York City and opened his own fancy dry goods store called R.H. Macy & Co in 1858—and the rest is history.

No vetting process guarantees flawless execution. But what is the alternative? If you don't try at all, that is guaranteed failure.

Don't complain that your job is a "grind" until you've exhausted absolutely every other possibility. Have you gone back to school? Have you leveraged your network for other opportunities? Have you considered starting your own business?

Those things take massive amounts of courage.

If your job is a grind, but your options for employment are limited, you can choose to be happy. That also takes courage. If the decision to be happy right where you are today is not enough, you can speak up. If that's still not enough, act!

If you see your position as a dead-end job, that is all it will ever be. But what if you dare to say, "This is not what I want. I am going to look for more."

No one is stuck doing anything. There is no armed guard standing behind your desk, forcing you to do your job. You don't *have* to do anything. Yes, you need to work, but you still have choices!

You can't just stay where you are and complain to anyone who will listen. That is the opposite of courage.

You're only limited by your fear. If you want a different job, get a better education or more training. If you want a better future, it's up to you, no one else.

COURAGE AT HOME

It's easy to see how courage can benefit you at work. It can open new doors and create fresh, exciting opportunities. But, how do you apply courage at home?

First of all, parents need a ton of courage! The easy road is to let kids do what they want, to threaten but never follow through. That's the lazy approach to parenting, but we've all seen it, time and time again.

You also need courage to communicate successfully with your significant other. It's easy to sweep things under the rug. Eventually, however, those little mounds under the rug will grow into bona fide mountains of resentment and deep-seated issues.

It takes courage to step up, and it takes practice. It also takes trust.

Home should be a safe place where you can talk about your greatest fears and wildest dreams, and know you are not being judged. It should actually be the most natural place to practice courage. People who love you unconditionally will recognize the courage it takes to be vulnerable, and they'll do whatever it takes to help you chase your dreams.

Unfortunately, there is a slew of societal norms and expectations that cause us to let fear reign, even in our safe place. Women are supposed to be natural nurturers and mothers. Men are supposed to be strong and not cry.

However, the most courageous people I know are willing to put themselves out there and be vulnerable. Brave wives and mothers can say, "I am overwhelmed and need help." Courageous husbands and dads can admit when they are afraid or cry when they need to cry.

If you feel courage is missing from your home, figure out what else is missing that may be causing fear to overpower courage. For example, is there a lack of vulnerability, routine, intention, communication, or accountability? Courage is what makes it all work, but if you don't have those other pieces in place, you can't act courageously.

Stand up and have the courage to say what is on your mind and to do the things that you really love. Courage, by extension, is confidence. Confident people don't let fear capture them and hold them hostage.

Have the confidence to be exactly who you are.

COURAGE HELPS YOU FIND YOUR PLACE

Two things tend to rule our lives more than anything else and stop us from acting with courage. The first is fear. The second one is not quite as obvious but just as powerful—it's our routines.

Does your routine help you achieve your goals or keep you from accomplishing them? It takes courage to look in the mirror and say, "This daily habit is keeping me from pursuing my passion."

What are you doing or not doing every day that is preventing you from winning? Changing your routine can be one of the most difficult things to do, but it may be necessary to experience a breakthrough.

What is one thing you could do today that scares you, but you know your hesitation about it is holding you back? Do it. Then do it again tomorrow. And the next day.

The more you do it, the more likely it will become a habit. The next thing you know, you won't even remember that person who was scared to take the first step toward what you really want out of life.

Everybody feels fear. You just need to decide not to let it defeat you. Decide every morning to be courageous.

People who live their lives freely act with courage every day—and isn't that what we all want? We crave the freedom to live our lives the way we want and to carve out our ideal existence.

Courage is what helps us find our place in the world.

What if you spoke your mind at work or at home? What if others knew how you felt? What if you took that terrifying but necessary first step toward something bigger and better?

How freeing would that be?

It just takes a little courage to start turning that into reality.

LET'S GO WIN

"Great dreams
of great dreamers are
always transcended."

A. P. J. ABDUL KALAM

Twelve

TRANSCENDENCE

No one is born with an inherent desire to fail. It doesn't matter how hard you may try; you'll never convince me that anyone is hard-wired to live a mediocre life of disappointment.

What happens to us over time is—thanks to a mix of harsh lessons, naysayers, and negative word speak—we start to question whether we are really meant for something great in this world.

It is these self-limiting beliefs and fears that stop people from being happy, that prevent people from believing they deserve to have what they want, or to be happy.

When we are young, we have big dreams. We want to be doctors, lawyers, firefighters, astronauts, superheroes. The majority of us end up with career titles that don't sound quite as extraordinary as "superhero" on our business cards, but dreams are still relevant and essential.

In fact, any significant thing that has ever happened or will happen started with a big dream.

Great dreamers are those who can dream beyond the limits of their imagination and who can think and live outside the box. However, the most influential world changers are not just *dreamers*; they are also *doers*. When big dreams are tied to planning and goal setting, that is when they become a reality.

This chapter is all about the final maxim of winning, one that is connected to dreaming big and trusting in the truth that you are meant for more.

I believe we are all meant for more—and the path to that place of abundance requires you to transcend.

To *transcend* is to travel outside the boundaries of your limiting beliefs. It requires you to reach beyond the apparent range of an idea or an expectation.

To rise above.

To seek and expect more and never settle for less.

It's about being ambitious, but it's also about being at peace with where you are. I realize that is a contradiction, but it turns out these two things are surprisingly symbiotic. Being happy with who you already are is the first step to transcending your self-limiting beliefs.

Next, recognize that what is holding you back is all just an illusion. Imagine a fence that is just high enough to prevent you from seeing what's on the other side. On the other side, barely out of sight and out of reach, is your best life. It's there. You can imagine what it's going to look like, even if you don't fully know.

What you do know is you want to get there.

That border you can't seem to cross? It's not even real! In your mind, you create so many boundaries, and it is those self-imposed restrictions that cause your heart and mind to be at war with each other.

STOP COMPROMISING

Have you built any walls in your mind that limit you? We all have. In particular, there is one particular type of boundary or limitation people place on their lives that must be transcended in order to win.

I call them compromises.

We compromise all the time—from making concessions at home or work to accepting less than what we want in a house or a vacation. More tragically, people often compromise in their relationships.

We are continually accepting less.

Another way to think of it is settling. It's saying things like, "I guess this apartment will do" or "I'm not as young or fit as I used to be, so I don't deserve to have an exciting relationship with someone I'm really attracted to."

I guess this is good enough.

Why settle for something that doesn't really make you happy? It's not about money or status. It's about belief. If you want it badly enough, it's yours. If you are willing to settle, it must not be significant enough to you.

Or, could it be that you don't believe you deserve to live a life of more?

People love to complain about their significant others. My question is always, "Have you talked to your spouse about what is bothering you?"

"Well, no. This is the way it has to be, so I'll just deal with it."

Maybe you believe if you brought up an issue, the relationship would crumble. I have news for you: If a little bit of honesty topples your relationship, it was not a real relationship. The real ones can weather the honesty and end up stronger and better as a result.

What if a few honest conversations created a fantastic relationship? Don't you deserve to find out? Stop compromising and start transcending and expecting more.

If you want more, one of the first things you need to do is stop listening to the stories in your head. Our self-limiting beliefs and biases are the most significant barriers to transcendent communication.

They are not reality. They are just what you've told yourself to be safe or to settle for what you've got.

Be unwilling to settle for what you think your fearful self deserves. If you want something, then who or what is standing in your way? Only you.

HELP OTHERS TRANSCEND

I was at a leadership retreat where I was honored to hear a speaker named Tom McCarthy. In 1986, famed self-help and success guru Anthony Robbins hired Tom as the first national sales leader and trainer for his Robbins Research sales force.

Tom rapidly became known for his ability to create transcendent relationships and connections. One of the most impactful lessons I learned from Tom is to stop letting the narratives we create in our heads limit our impact with others.

Here is what Tom does to take control of his life and transcend—and by extension, give others the love and encouragement they need to transcend as well. Tom makes it a point to share love and support with another person three times a day. It could be someone he hasn't spoken to in years. The point is not to ask, "What's in it for me?" but to send positive energy out to another human being.

He told us, "I'm not looking for anything in return, and yet, it's amazing how often a simple, heartfelt note will open a door that has been closed for years."

This idea really hit home with me. Why settle for stagnant relationships when you can make real connections and have a more sincere, loving life? In most cases, it takes less than five minutes and consists of nothing more than, "I just wanted you to know I was thinking about you and how amazing you are. Have a great day."

Can you imagine receiving such a note? I don't know about you, but that kind of message would make my day, maybe even my week or month.

When I got home from the retreat, I took myself out of my comfort zone and tried it out. I hadn't talked to Andy, a friend, and former colleague, in over five years, but I sent him a text that read, "Hey man, I know it's been a long time, but I was thinking about you. And I just wanted to tell you what an awesome impact you have had on my life."

Andy replied almost instantly with, "JM, I'm so glad you reached out! I've thought about you many times over the years. We need to reconnect."

Maybe we will end up rekindling our friendship, or perhaps we will go another few years in between texts. The key point is I made a positive impact on Andy's day.

We lie to ourselves continually. We say things like, "It would be too awkward to reach out after all these years."

We assume that everybody's "all set" and that they have plenty of friends and encouragement, but this is rarely true! We all need more. And we all need to give more of it out.

Why not give that to people and help others transcend? You have nothing to lose and so much to gain.

DARE TO FAIL

You may feel stuck in an unfulfilling job right now. We've all been there.

Do you believe you are meant for more?

Well, you are.

If you don't like what you do, speak up. What if you told your boss, "Hey, I'd like to throw my hat in the ring to become the marketing manager."

What if you went back to school for the degree you need to do your dream job?

What. If.

A transcendent existence is a life of pursuing the "what if." It takes tremendous courage even to begin to think you are meant for more. Your boss could shoot you down. Your spouse could say, "Sorry, hon. We can't afford to send you back to school."

Don't let someone else write your story. Transcend.

We get labels attached to us, and we start to believe them. Somebody says, "You're not a great public speaker," and you begin to think it's true. You are constantly being judged and labeled, but it's up to you to decide to believe them or not.

What do you want? Forget what restraints you think you have, or what labels people have given you. Maybe somebody discouraged you or said you weren't good enough, and you believed them. Don't let the limiting beliefs of simple or jealous minds hold you back.

Walt Disney's ideas and even his cartoons were initially shot down by others. He got fired as an illustrator in his early career because he "lacked imagination." Good thing he didn't believe the haters, right? Imagine for a moment if he had.

Imagine a world without Walt Disney. No Magic Kingdom. No Mickey Mouse.

Sounds awful.

If you ask a 5-year-old if they could be a professional athlete or an astronaut or the President of the United States one day, they won't hesitate to say, "Yes!"

At some point, people start to convince us we can't, and we lose our ability to transcend those limiting beliefs. I want you to tap back into that 5-year-old part of you—the visionary, the believer, the dreamer.

If you want to be a movie star, why wouldn't you try? What's the worst thing that could happen? You don't become a movie star. But what's the best thing that could happen? You fulfill your dream!

Adventurer Norman Vaughan said, "Dream big and dare to fail." If you go after something with everything you have and still fail, you are not a failure. You are an absolute inspiration!

When my son was four, he wanted to be a professional baseball player. The odds of that happening are slim—but he never heard that statistic from his dad. I told him to pursue that dream with everything he had.

I give my kids every assurance that dreams can come true, but those dreams do require you to give 100 percent of your efforts. Otherwise, you'll always live with regret and be doomed to live in the past, reliving the "glory days" in your mind.

Don't be like the old high school football hero, with his high school trophy sitting next to the TV and his "remember when" stories.

Give 100 percent and feel great about that—win or lose. If you fail, you go on to climb the next mountain with your head held high.

YOU WERE CREATED TO WIN

Maybe you feel like you have every reason not to win.

Maybe you weren't set up for success in life due to circumstances beyond your control in childhood or young adulthood.

That is not your fault.

But it *is* all the more reason to transcend.

If you're really passionate about manifesting something, whether it's a meaningful life, fulfilling career, or blissful marriage, just go for it. That doesn't mean you're going to succeed. In fact, likely there are many times you won't.

But give 100 percent, and life will favor you with joy and gratification.

Christopher Reeve became famous in the 1970s and 1980s for playing the indomitable superhero we all know and love called Superman. The Man of Steel. A real sight to behold! He ushered in the era of movie stars doing extreme workouts to build real muscles for a role rather than wearing a muscle suit.

At the height of his career, Reeve was thrown from a horse and became a quadriplegic. He lived the rest of his days in a wheelchair and could not even breathe on his own. He used a portable ventilator to breathe until the day he passed.

If you went from being the Man of Steel to needing someone to feed you, bathe you, clothe you, and wipe you, do you think you'd be able to transcend and go on to live a full life? Reeve did. He tirelessly lobbied on behalf of people with injuries like his and became the face and voice of human embryonic stem cell research.

In a speech one day, Reeve said, "Your body is not who you are. The mind and spirit transcend the body."

Superman got it. He knew the secret. There are no limitations but the ones we place on ourselves. That's truly all that is holding us back.

There are more than 7.5 billion people in the world, but most of them just exist. They work at a job they don't enjoy, and they trudge through life and dread the small things (which is most things).

It takes no courage, vulnerability, or authenticity to join the crowd. It takes very little energy to complain and to settle. It takes something special to transcend, to stand alone with confidence and pride.

You can't achieve any great thing by following the path of the majority. People choose that path when they don't have their own dreams, and they can't make their own way.

Transcendent dreamers are those who believe in creating their opportunities, not stumbling across them.

The fear of failure will always be there. Let that fear remind you that you are on the right path. Without fear and doubt, there is no courage, and there is no transcendence.

If you want to build something great, it will require patience, time, courage, and all of the traits we discussed in this book.

There is no faking greatness.

There is no faking happiness.

There is no faking courage.

Be your real, authentic self, surround yourself with people who believe in you, who will hold you accountable, and who will refuse to put you in a box with a static label.

Actively pursue your best life, right here, right now. Pursue it knowing that it is not a stagnant destination somewhere in the distance.

Each morning, each hour, and each minute that you are alive, life is meant to be pursued with mindful intention, set around positive routines, and of course, fun! The moment you stop doing that is the moment you let life call the shots rather than the other way around.

The person I am today is not the same person I was yesterday. I plan to continue to grow and change tomorrow as well.

You are blessed with unique gifts in this life, one or more areas where you shine and add value and purpose to the people around you, the community, and the world. You were created as an unrepeatable miracle, and you are destined for greatness.

You were absolutely created to win. Let's go win!

AUTHOR BIO

JM RYERSON is an entrepreneur who has been building companies and leading sales teams for more than 16 years. He is the chief leadership officer and managing vice president of Appreciation Financial. JM is also the co-founder and CEO of Let's Go Win, a company dedicated to helping people around the world live their best lives. He has spent his career focused on enriching the lives of others while continuing to educate himself on best practices in leadership, vulnerability, and teamwork.

JM's great passion is helping his team members lead a life of fulfillment and become vulnerable and open to what life has in store for them. His ultimate goal is to give others the tools that will allow them to transcend their self-limiting beliefs. To JM, there is nothing more inspiring than to watch someone achieve more than they could ever imagine. That is why he considers it a real privilege to be even a small part of people's incredible journeys. JM lives in Granite Bay, California, with his wife, Lisa, and their two amazing boys.

NEXT STEPS

Did you know you can book JM to speak at your next corporate event or training?

His audiences love his authentic style and laid-back delivery that is guaranteed to entertain, motivate, and encourage. If you are looking for a speaker who will inspire you and fire up your team to win, contact us today for more information.

Maybe you are looking for a more one-on-one approach to winning. If you are ready to take your life and your career to the next level, talk to JM today about personalized coaching and mentoring.

Bulk discounts are also available for the book. Grab a copy for everyone in your organization. They make great Christmas gifts!

WWW.LETSGOWIN.COM

Made in the USA
Coppell, TX
07 January 2022

71005631R00103